STUDENT TEACHING, CLASSROOM MANAGEMENT, AND PROFESSIONALISM

Edited by
Wm. Ray Heitzmann
Villanova University
Charles Staropoli
University of Delaware

MSS INFORMATION CORPORATION

Distributed by **ARNO PRESS**
3 Park Avenue, New York, N.Y. 10016

This is a custom-made book of readings prepared for the courses taught by the editors, as well as for related courses and for college and university libraries. For information about our program, please write to:

MSS INFORMATION CORPORATION

MSS wishes to express its appreciation to the authors of the articles in this collection for their cooperation in making their work available in this format.

Library of Congress Cataloging in Publication Data

Heitzmann, William Ray, comp.
  Student teaching, classroom management, and professionalism.

  A collection of articles previously published in various journals.
    1. Student teaching — Addresses, essays, lectures.
  2. Classroom management — Addresses, essays, lectures.
  3. Teaching as a profession — Addresses, essays, lectures.   I. Staropoli, Charles, joint comp.   II. Title.
  LB2157.A3H38 1974   370'.733   73-18119
  ISBN 0-8422-5143-X
  ISBN 0-8422-0367-2 (pbk.)

CONTENTS

PREFACE

Undergraduate teacher-education programs serve to educate as well as train students. Candidates pursue general academic subjects (fine arts, social sciences, languages) as well as education courses which serve to educate as well as train. While some education courses contribute more to the learner's cultural knowledge (philosophy of education, history of educational thought, comparative educational systems) most education courses contribute to training the learner for his or her profession — the student teaching course is certainly paramount in this regard. Designed to be the culminating experience of a teacher-training program it enables the student teacher to "put it all together." This is a unique opportunity provided to the education major to "practice teach" prior to entering the profession.

The enclosed articles related to "Student Teaching," "Classroom Management" and "Professionalism" are designed to increase the reader's cognitive and affective knowledge and consequently result in a successful practicum. The editors have carefully chosen the readings to aid the student teacher to obtain the finest teaching experience possible. This is a period of exploration and experimentation — the student teacher with the encouragement and support of the cooperating teacher and the university supervisor should utilize several successful instructional strategies in the classroom. With a dedication to the profession and a commitment to maximizing student learning, initial fears will quickly dissolve into a routine of imaginative planning and creative direction of student activities, resulting in efficient and successful student learning.

STUDENT TEACHING

Humanizing Teacher Education

By Robert Blume

There is no single method of teaching which can be demonstrated to be superior for all teachers. Nor will knowledge about good teaching insure superior performance. These findings from research conducted over the past 10 years have thrown teacher education into a dilemma. If not knowledge and methods, what shall we have our prospective teachers learn in college?

A study published in 1961 by the National Education Association, in which all of the research available on good and poor teaching was reviewed, failed to find any method of teaching which was clearly superior to all others.

At about the same time, Combs and Soper conducted research with good and poor teachers to determine if the good ones knew better than the poor ones the characteristics of a good helping relationship.[1] They found no significant difference between the knowledge of the two categories of teachers.

What does distinguish between good and poor teachers? Certainly we all think we can tell the difference, but does research bear out our beliefs?

Twenty years ago a startling finding came out of a study of various styles of psychotherapy. At that time the psychoanalysts and the Rogerians were debating whether it was more effective for the therapist to be direct and forceful in dealing with his client, or whether the client should be encouraged to think out his own solutions to problems while the therapist assumes a client-centered role.

Fiedler found that expert therapists, no matter what school of thought they belonged to, tended to advocate the same kind of relationship with their clients. In fact, these experts were more alike in their beliefs about the therapeutic relationship than were the beginners and experts in the same school. This relationship has come to be called "the helping relationship."

Combs and Soper modified the questions Fiedler used with the therapists, in order to make them appropriate for educators, and administered the instrument to a group of expert classroom teachers. They found that these teachers agreed with the expert therapists about the relationship which was most desirable and productive for

PHI DELTA KAPPAN, March 1971, pp. 411-415.

8

helpers and helpees.

As mentioned above, when they asked poor teachers the same questions, they found that they, too, knew the answers. They concluded that a good helping relationship is something most people know about, but not all are capable of practicing.

With these questions in mind — "What does make a difference in the ability of teachers to practice the good helping relationship?" and "What shall we have future teachers learn in college?" — let us turn to some of the recent criticism of the schools.

The new critics (as opposed to the all testify to the failure of the school to educate people in a way that gives them a feeling of dignity and an understanding of their world.

Some consider this indictment too harsh. They hold that the school can't be blamed for all of society's ills. Whether or not the school is responsible for causing our problems, it is the institution responsible for producing educated people, who will in turn make the wise decisions, both large and small, that will gradually improve life. Unfortunately, we are not moving in this direction now; on the contrary, life is becoming more grim and joyless all the time, and therefore the school *is* vulnerable to the above charge.

Education must include more than the acquisition of a few more facts and a faster reading rate. It must be the instrument through which people release the tremendous creative potential that was born into all of us. Whatever methods and materials are needed to do the job — that is education.

But this isn't enough. We must also help our young to develop compassion, concern for others, faith in themselves, the ability to think critically, the ability to love, the ability to cooperate with others, the ability to maintain good health, and, above all, the ability to remain open to other people and new experiences. This is *humanistic* education.

In order to achieve this kind of school we must abandon the old patterns along with the old assumptions, and search together for a concept of education that will in Jourard's words "turn on and awaken more people to expanded perspectives of the world, new challenges, possible ways to experience the world and our own embodied being." We *can* create educational patterns that are much more exciting than anything we adults have experienced in our elementary or secondary schooling. The University of Florida has begun a program of elementary teacher education which is a radical departure from those of the past. This program has abolished courses and regularly scheduled classes, replacing them with individual study and small discussion groups. Each student becomes a member of a seminar led by the same faculty member for the two years he is enrolled in the program. Students have the opportunity to work with children every week, and almost every day, from the beginning of their teacher education to the end.

This program is based on principles which have emerged in educational literature over the past two decades, and more specifically on extensive research which Arthur Combs and his associates have conducted at the University of Florida. These principles are:

○ People do only what they would rather do (from Freud). That is, people behave according to choices they make from among alternatives they see available to them at the moment.

○ Learning has two aspects: 1) acquiring new information, and 2) discovering the *personal meaning* of that information. Information itself is useless. Only when individuals find the link between specific information and their own lives are they able to put it to use. This principle is not well understood by educators. Most of our efforts to improve education involve new ways to deliver information to people. Very few innovations involve helping learners to discover the personal meaning of that information.

O It is more appropriate for people to learn a few concepts rather than many facts.

O Learning is much more efficient if the learner first feels a need to know that which is to be learned. This principle has been known for a long time, but the response of educators to it has been to artificially "motivate" students with letter grades and other rewards. None of these schemes works as well as the genuine desire to learn, and in fact they frequently get in the way of that desire by substituting artificial for real motivation.

O No one specific item of information, and no specific skill, is essential for effective teaching. Any one fact or skill that could be mentioned might be missing in a very effective teacher. Furthermore, it would be presumptuous for teacher educators in the 1970's, drawing on their experience in the 40's, 50's, and 60's, to declare certain teaching skills or knowledge essential for teachers in the 80's, and 90's, and beyond. We just don't know what the job of the teacher will be in 20 years, or even 10. Hopefully it will be quite different from what it is today.

O People learn more easily and rapidly if they help make the important decisions about their learning.

O People learn and grow more quickly if they aren't afraid to make mistakes. They can be creative only if they can risk making errors.

O Objectivity is a valuable asset for a researcher, but it is not very useful for workers in the helping professions, such as teaching. What is needed instead is the opposite of objectivity — concern and caring. As Jack Frymier has said, we want students not only to know about cold, hard facts, but to have some "hot feelings about hard facts." We must produce teachers who have developed strong values about teaching.

O Teachers teach the way they have been taught — not the way they have been taught to teach. If we want elementary and secondary teachers to be warm, friendly people who relate positively and openly with their students, then we must treat them that way in our college programs. We must respect our teacher education students if we expect them to respect their pupils.

O Pressure on students produces negative behaviors, such as cheating, avoidance, fearfulness, and psychosomatic illness. Students tend to become more closed in their interpersonal relationships when they are pressured.

O Our teachers would be more effective if they were self-actualizers. Teachers ideally should be more healthy than "normal" people. They should be creative, self-motivated, well-liked persons.

In his book, *The Professional Education of Teachers,* Arthur Combs reviews "third force psychology," the alternative to the Freudian and stimulus-response theories which have dominated our educational thought for the past half century. Three basic principles of perceptual psychology are significant for humanistic education:

1. All behavior of an individual is the direct result of his field of perceptions at the moment of his behaving.

2. The most important perceptions an individual has are those he has about himself. The self-concept is the most important single influence affecting an individual's behavior.

3. All individuals have a basic need for personal adequacy. We all behave in ways which will, according to our view of the situation, lead to our self enhancement. Once aware of this fundamental drive toward growth and improvement, we can see that it is unnecessary to reward a child to encourage him to learn. If he already wants to learn, we need only help him, by giving him the environment which makes it easy and the materials which are appropriate for the kind of learning toward which he is motivated. We need to become aware of his motivation and plan learning experiences which will fit into it. The role of the teacher, then, is that of facilitator, encourager, helper, assister, colleague, and friend of his students.

Teaching is therefore a helping relationship rather than a command relationship. It is similar to counseling, psychotherapy, nursing, human relations work, social work, and many other helping professions.

A number of studies have been conducted at the University of Florida which have investigated the nature of the helping relationship. Combs and others have studied counselors, teachers, Episcopal priests, nurses, and college teachers to see if the more effective practitioners in these fields have different ways of perceiving than do the ineffective ones. The perceptual organizations of these professionals were examined in great detail in the following four categories:

Category 1: *The general perceptual organization.* Is he more interested in people or things? Does he look at people from the outside, or does he try to see the world as they see it? Does he look for the reasons people behave as they do in the here and now, or does he try to find historical reasons for behavior?

Category 2: *Perceptions of other people.* Does he see people generally as able to do things or unable? As friendly or unfriendly? As worthy or unworthy? As dependable or undependable?

Category 3: *Perceptions of self.* Does he see himself as with people or apart from them? As able or unable? As dependable or undependable? As worthy or unworthy? As wanted or unwanted?

Category 4: *Perceptions of the professional task.* Does he see his job as one of freeing people or controlling them? Does he see his role as one of revealing or concealing? As being involved or uninvolved? As encouraging process or achieving goals?

The results of these studies consistently indicated that the effective helpers saw people from the inside rather than the outside. They were more sensitive to the feelings of students. They were more concerned with people than things. They saw behavior as caused by the here-and-now perceptions, rather than by historical events. They saw others and themselves as able, worthy, and dependable; they saw their task as freeing rather than controlling, and as involved, revealing, and encouraging process.

As mentioned above, one significant finding of these studies was that objectivity had a *negative* correlation with effectiveness as a helper. For example, the teacher who observes two boys fighting and tries to "get to

11

the bottom of the problem" by asking how it started, what led up to the first blow being struck, etc., is not helping as effectively as the teacher in a similar situation who says, "Mike, I can see you are very angry with David and you want to hurt him, but I can't let you do that. How do you feel, David? Are you mad too?" The latter teacher is not being so objective; he isn't trying to place the blame logically on one boy or the other. Instead he is trying to show the two boys that he recognizes the way they feel *at this moment,* and he wants them to know that he is a friend of each of them and will help them to express their feelings. Violence is usually an attempt to express strong feelings. The best helpers are those who help people to express these feelings without violence.

The implications of this research are important for the Florida New Elementary Program. For example, if good teachers are more sensitive to the feelings of students, we should provide more opportunities for teacher education students to enter into more personal, meaningful relationships with other students, faculty, and children. If effective teachers see others as able, well-intentioned, and dependable, they need a warm, friendly, cooperative atmosphere in which to interact with children and in-service teachers during their teacher education. If the effective teacher sees himself as able, likable, and dependable, he must be treated as a person of worth, dignity, and integrity from the very beginning of his professional program. Finally, if effective teachers see the teaching task as one of freeing and assisting, rather than controlling or coercing, we must provide teacher education which does not insist on particular methods, but which encourages students to seek

their own best methods. These programs themselves should encompass a wide variety of approaches. The instructors will need to be concerned with the attitudes and perceptions of teachers, not merely with subject matter and methods.

Various members of the College of Education saw a challenge in this research and in the book Combs published in 1965. They decided to build a new program for the preparation of elementary teachers. This program consists of three parts: the seminar, the substantive panel, and field experience.

The seminar is the heart of the program. It is here most of all that the student develops a close relationship with a faculty member, one who knows him well over the entire period of his professional program. He also becomes a member of a small group of students. Thirty students are assigned to each of the three seminar leaders. They range from beginners, who have just come into the program, to seniors, who have completed all but the final phases of their work. When a student graduates, a new one is taken in to replace him. The 30 students are divided into two groups of 15 for discussion purposes, and each small group meets for two hours per week. These meetings are for the purpose of discussing everything which comes to the minds of the students and their leader relative to education. More specifically, the purpose is the discovery of the personal meaning of the information and experiences which the students are encountering in the other aspects of the program.

The seminar leader serves as advisor to each of the 30 students in his group. He is responsible for helping them schedule outside course work and for keeping the records of their work within the program. He also conducts evaluation activities for his group in the form of weekly activity sheets and the midpoint and final review conferences.

The second aspect is the substantive panel. It includes faculty members who normally teach methods, foundations, and curriculum courses. Included are math, reading, language arts, social studies, science, art, social foundations, psychological foundations, curriculum, black studies, and testing and research. In each of these areas the faculty member distributes lists of competencies for students to complete and hand in, or to discuss in faculty-student conferences. The competencies range over the entire area of didactic learnings within each of the fields mentioned. Certain competencies are required, while others are optional. In the area of curriculum, for example, there are four required competencies, and each student must do three more from a list of seven optional ones. Even the required competencies may be done in two different ways, thus carrying through the idea of giving students wide latitude for choice making. Some of the competencies involve working with a small group of children and writing a critique. The students do these while they are involved in their field experience. Others include reading in the library and writing papers summarizing the literature, or reacting to it. Students are encouraged to design their own competencies as alternatives to some of the optional ones. They write out a contract form for this purpose. The faculty member signs the contract when he has approved the design, and again when the competency has been completed. Substantive panel members conduct some small-group sessions each week to help students develop the understanding needed to complete the competencies. Students are free to sign up for these meetings or not as they choose, but if they sign up they are expected to attend. These meetings are usually offered as a series of three or four. Some competencies consist of passing a test over material which has been presented in these small-group meetings.

Obviously, the student can't work in all substantive areas at once. He must choose which three or four he will work on each quarter, depending on his schedule of field experiences and outside classes. With this much freedom and responsibility, there is danger that students who have been spoon-fed all of their lives will goof off and get behind in their completion of the competencies. We feel this is a calculated risk worth taking, in order to gain the advantages of having students feel free to explore and probe in directions dictated by their growing interest in becoming teachers.

The field experience aspect of the program begins with level one, which consists of tutoring an individual child and observing classrooms in the Gainesville area. The student and his advisor decide when he has had enough observation experience — usually about 10 one-hour observations. The tutoring continues for an entire quarter. In level two, the student is designated "teacher assistant." He does whatever needs to be done — work with individual children or small groups, or even record keeping. Teacher assistants spend a minimum of six hours per week in the classroom. In level three, the student is designated "teacher associate." He now accepts more responsibility for planning and teaching certain groups of children within the class, or certain aspects of the curriculum for the whole class. As teacher associate he teaches two hours every day. Eventually he must do an intensive period of teaching, level four, which requires full time in the classroom for five weeks.

One of the unique aspects of this program is the flexibility of time requirements. The program is expected to take six quarters to complete, but a student who wants to push harder can complete it in as little as four quarters. The student who needs more time to finish, or to develop confidence or maturity, might take a longer period of time. This is as it should be, we feel. If we seriously believe in individual differences in learners, we must make provision for people to go through our program at different rates.

The evaluation of each student's work within the program is handled by the seminar leader, the student himself, and the members of the substantive panel. The student completes competencies in each substantive area, and they are evaluated by the panel member. He rates them on a pass-fail basis and checks them off as the student completes his list for his area. He sends a list of the competencies completed to the seminar leader who keeps the student's records.

Approximately half-way through the program each student has a midpoint evaluation, during which he goes over his progress with the seminar leader and one member of the substantive panel. The number of competencies completed in each area, the number yet to be done, and the field experiences to date are all discussed, and a proposed timetable for completion of the program is written down in his folder. When the student has completed all of the requirements he sits for a final review in the same way, and it is determined if he is ready to teach. The seminar leader is aware of each student's progress each quarter, because he keeps all of the records, and

he receives feedback from other faculty members who have observations about particular students.

One of the strongest features of the program is the participation of students in every phase of decision making. The students feel ownership in the program as a result of being on various faculty-student committees, such as a committee to write a handbook for new students, a committee to evaluate the competencies in the various substantive areas, or a committee to plan next term's schedule. Each seminar sends a representative to the bi-weekly staff meetings, not only to observe and report back, but to participate in the discussions as a full-fledged member of the group.

Within one year, two very significant, student-initiated changes were made in the program. The group petitioned the dean of the College of Education to place the entire program on a pass-fail basis rather than the letter-grading system then in use. Their logic was persuasive and the change was made.

In another case, a small group of students asked for some academic preparation for teaching in integrated schools. They were all having some teaching experience in schools that were predominantly black, and they recognized their own lack of background for teaching in those classrooms. This suggestion was followed by the creation of a faculty-student committee, which eventually planned a black-studies program and received some limited funding for its operation.

Whether students learn as much about teaching here as they would in a more standard program will have to be determined by the research which is under way at the present time, but several perceptions are generally shared by the staff members who work most closely with these future teachers. One perception is that the students leave our campus with a solid feeling of confidence about their ability to teach.

A fact which pleases the staff is that *many* of our students ask for an intensive teaching assignment in a school which has large numbers of disadvantaged children. It isn't clear just why this is happening, but it reflects the kind of attitudes we hope to see students developing.

One coed who was having her final review conference said, "It took me almost a year in this program before I felt like these ideas were mine — and then it was easy after that." That statement summarizes what this program is trying to do: not merely to have students *learn about* principles of humanistic education, but to have them feel that they are *their* ideas.

The specific elements of the Florida New Elementary Program are still evolving, and will continue to evolve. What is more important, we believe, are the ideas on which they are based. These principles are valid for humanistic education at any level. We hope to introduce them into elementary classrooms by preparing teachers in ways that are consistent with those principles, because teachers teach the way they were taught.

---

[1]More information concerning this study and others cited here can be found in A. W. Combs, *et al., Florida Studies in the Helping Professions*, Social Science Monograph No. 37. Gainesville, Fla.: University of Florida Press, 1969.

THE ELEMENTARY TEACHER PREPARATION PROGRAM:
A GRADUATED CLINICAL APPROACH TO
THE EDUCATION SEQUENCE

Ray Heitzmann
Chuck Staropoli

Unfortunately, for many years education courses in some teacher training programs have been taught in a manner that have totally divorced the future practitioner from children. Both students and teachers have reacted to this artificial situation which treats theory alone and does not attempt to integrate it with practice or reality. The result has been to attach to methods courses a clinical component. While this may be an improvement, a developmental or graduated approach would certainly be more desirable educationally.

In view of the above, the University of Delaware has introduced into its elementary teacher education program the concept of graduated clinical responsibilities. This program is based upon the medical model.

The program begins in the sophomore year when the education sequence commences. As a sophomore, the student takes the following courses: Psychological Foundations of Education, Sociological Foundations of Education, and Historical Foundations of Philosophical Foundations of Education. As part of these courses, the student will observe various instructional and administrative organizations of educational systems and community social agencies. The student engages in limited participation as an instructional aide and as a tutor. Finally there is a psychological, sociological, and philosophical or historical analysis of the various participation and observation experiences by the students. The sophomores have a choice of the settings for their participation — urban, suburban, or rural.

During the junior year, there are eight methods courses (twenty four credits) taken by the elementary education major — art, language arts, mathematics, music, physical education, reading, science, and social studies. For administrative convenience, these courses (which meet daily for an hour and a half each) are grouped together in blocks of two and taken for seven weeks each. These courses have a strong clinical component as four of the seven weeks weeks are spent at a cooperating school. After the students gain a knowledge of a structure of the discipline, and the materials and methods to impart it, they then engage in tutoring, small group instruction, and large group instruction at the schools to which they are assigned, under the supervision of co-operating teachers and university faculty. The cooperating schools vary according to environment: urban, suburban, rural, and administrative and instructional organization.

Thus, prior,to student teaching, the pre-service teacher has had several experiences working with young students in various settings and has had

ORIGINAL MANUSCRIPT, 1973.

the opportunity to plan lessons and units and field test them in a classroom situation. These experiences not only serve as a screening device for the College of Education, but enable the college student to choose a student teaching arrangement that will maximize the possibility of success.

During the senior year, the students engage in the extended student teaching experience. During this time, under the supervision of the college supervisor and the cooperating teacher, the student's experience expands into a full teaching program enabling the senior elementary education major to operate as a classroom teacher.

The graduated clinical approach to education courses provides many benefits to participating schools as well as to university faculty and students. All clinical experiences are coordinated by the Office of Clinical Studies which, in some respects, is difficult administratively. However, the benefits far outweigh any minor logistic problems. Although the program is in its initial stages, feedback from students, faculty, and cooperating districts has been very positive.

STUDENT TEACHING:
THE CULMINATING EXPERIENCE

Philip S. Fox

STUDY after study has shown that student teaching is the most functional and practical experience included in the education of prospective teachers. Teachers with years of experience consistently rate student teaching as the most valuable part of all preservice education. The supervised teaching experience is the culmination of the preservice program of future teachers. This aspect of teacher education is so important that even greater attention should be given it in the preparation of teachers than has been given in the past.

The contrast between what was offered to future teachers in our early normal schools and what is being offered today in our better teacher preparation institutions is great. One experience, however, has been constant —"practice in teaching." Student teaching in the past was limited to the classroom and the schoolhouse, but provisions can be found in accounts of the earliest normal schools that gave prominence to this experience. In the first state-supported teacher-training institution, established in Berlin in 1788, student teaching was a part of the professional training.

The meaning and application of practice teaching has expanded through the years. Its very title has changed with its growing meaning and expanding implications for teacher education. Student teaching has evolved through the years from such titles as "plans of exercises," "teaching exercises," "practice in teaching," "directed teaching," and "responsible teaching."

The pattern of today has grown from "teaching exercises" in which students played the part of pupils to the present student teaching experiences that provide the student with all the contacts and experiences that a regular teacher has in and out of the classroom. In the past, limitations prevented the student teachers from going beyond the classroom and resulted in an incomplete picture of future responsibilities. Now, in many localities, student teaching not only includes full-time responsible teaching but also involves living among pupils and other teachers in the total school and community environment.

A new approach added to the previous stages of student teaching has been termed professional laboratory

JOURNAL OF HEALTH, PHYSICAL EDUCATION AND RECREATION, April 1964, Vol. 35, pp. 39-40, 88-89.

18

experiences. These include the instructional functions of a teacher and also the important tasks involved in the non-instructional functions.

This new approach to student teaching provides experiences in the classroom and experiences with forces outside of the classroom that act on the pupil. These give breadth and depth to the present-day concept of student teaching.

Student teaching as it is used in this article is the period of guided teaching when the prospective teacher takes increasing responsibility for the teaching-learning process with a given group of pupils over a consecutive period of time, usually more than six weeks. The term includes actual teaching and those non-teaching functions usually performed by the teacher.

The phrase "of guided teaching" implies that the student teacher is under supervision. This guidance should be under the joint responsibility of the cooperating teacher and supervising college personnel. The cooperating teacher is a member of the faculty of the cooperating school and is recognized by the teacher education institution as qualified to guide a group of pupils, plus one or more student teachers, guiding them in their understanding and teaching of the given pupil group. Supervising college personnel are the members of the faculty of the teacher education institution who visit the student in his teaching-learning situation and advise him in his program of professional laboratory experiences.

Professional laboratory experiences should be an integral part of the total program for the preparation of teachers. The entire preparation of the prospective teacher should be so inter-related that it all contributes to the student's success as a beginning teacher. The student teaching experience should be viewed as a part of, and not something apart from, the rest of the future teacher's preparation.

The expanding point of view concerning student teaching is changing many aspects of the over-all picture. Several of the more significant trends and innovations in student teaching are:

1. Increase in the amount of student teaching required for both elementary and secondary education.
2. Provision of time for regular two- and three-way conferences between college supervisors, cooperating teachers, and student teachers.
3. Participation of academic college personnel in the supervision of student teachers.
4. Requirement of participating work experiences with children before the student teaching experience.
5. Utilization of a professional core program prior to student teaching.
6. Development of a seminar during and following student teaching to discuss problems that grow out of student teaching.
7. Inauguration of an internship with supervision by the teacher preparation institution.
8. Requirement of a balanced program of general education prior to professional preparation.
9. Utilization of a cumulative fold about the student teacher to plan his student teaching experience.
10. Provisions for student teaching experience in underprivileged areas as well as in more privileged neighborhoods.

Student teaching experience should bridge the gap between theory and practice. It should be an aspect of the total preservice program during which the prospective teacher can determine and crystalize his educational principles and philosophy, and when he can put to test the ideas learned in the pro-

Objectives for Student Teaching as Indicated by District of Columbia Teachers College Senior Students	Number of Times Reported
1. Become acquainted with and understand pupils	48
2. Gain self confidence	45
3. Plan and carry out unit plans	40
4. Secure experience in managing a class	40
5. Find if I am fitted for teaching	37
6. Understand the teacher's responsibility	33
7. Better understanding of the teacher's job	30
8. Improve my philosophy of teaching	21
9. Develop my personality	20
10. Opportunity to work with other teachers	17

fessional and academic classes. This period of concentrated student teaching provides the student with the chance to ask and, perhaps, answer the following questions: Do I understand what the theories mean in application? Does the theory work? It is the student's opportunity to discover his strong points as well as weak points. He attempts to achieve good teaching through planning, teaching-observing, evaluation, and conferring.

All of these purposes should be accomplished with the assistance and guidance of college faculty staff members and cooperating school and community personnel. During this period of experiencing the activities of a full-time teacher, all of the supervising personnel should be eager and ready to help the student teacher become proficient and competent.

A wide variety of activities is needed to assure that the prospective teacher may have the best possible foundation for future success. To bring practice and theory together and to integrate the whole teacher-education program, the better programs of professional preparation provide for a variety of student teaching. experiences, including teaching, attending faculty meetings, sharing in commu-nity activities, and sharing, or assuming, teacher responsibilities. This broadening concept of student teaching calls for the student to participate actively in the major functions of the teacher — in the classroom, in the community, and in the total school organization and administration.

Many challenging and worthwhile experiences outside the classroom need to be provided. The thoughtful and well-directed student teacher will take advantage of as many non-instructional experiences as possible. Recent graduates of a teacher preparation institution enumerated the following out-of-classroom experiences while student teaching:

Helped with the screening for the health examination
Organized class picnics and outings
Repaired athletic equipment
Guided the cheer leaders
Organized and supervised playground activities
Visited homes
Attended meetings of many civic and community organizations
Organized an early morning class in physical fitness
Participated in a faculty-parent intra-mural program
Worked with less skilled children after school
Helped inventory school supplies

Planned and organized a tumbling assembly
Visited health agencies
Helped with First Aid
Organized athletic clubs
Conducted a week end school camping program
Offered guidance to pupils
Presented a program at the PTA meeting
Organized and supervised intramurals
Helped coach varsity teams

What are the objectives of the students in student teaching? This question was answered in part by a questionnaire submitted to the senior students in student teaching? This ques-Teachers College. At the beginning of the senior year the students were asked, as a result of their experiences in observation of teaching and other professional preparation, to indicate their objectives for student teaching. The table on this page shows a list of ten objectives which were reported most often by a group of fifty senior students.

Surveys made by the author have indicated the importance of developing good human relations during the student teaching experience. It has been shown many times that patience and understanding are considered by pupils as the qualities they desire most in their teachers. Among the characteristics of teachers liked best, indications are that pupils prefer a teacher who is democratic. Prospective teachers should be given the opportunity to acquire this characteristic as they prepare for the teaching profession; a prospective teacher becomes democratic by living democratically and experiencing student teaching in a learning climate that is democratic.

If these purposes and objectives of the student teaching experience are to be realized, teacher preparation institutions must provide the prospective teacher with superior guidance and supervision. To a large measure, the key to a successful experience in student teaching is cooperative and understanding supervision. If supervision is not adequate, or is done by faculty members especially skillful in methodology and class control, the student teaching experience loses much of its effectiveness.

Factors of importance in the realization of the purposes of student teaching and guidelines to a successful student teaching experience are as follows:

1. Supervising and cooperating personnel should view the student teacher as a growing person rather than as an accomplished, perfect teacher.

2. The college faculty member, the cooperating teacher, and the student should cooperatively establish what the student is going to try to accomplish in his student experience.

3. The classroom experience of the student teacher should be constantly evaluated in terms of what is happening to children.

4. First contacts for the student teacher should be in settings akin in point of view to the theory in the college. The student teacher and cooperating teacher should have somewhat similar educational points of view and philosophy in the first contact period.

5. It may be desirable in later student teaching contacts to place the student in a situation in which the point of view is diametrically opposed to his point of view.

6. Student teaching should be scheduled before the senior year, so that many of the new problems of the student may be referred back to subject matter and theory courses.

7. The individual student should move into his student teaching as fast as possible. The readiness of the student for student teaching should be based upon the best judgment of the student

himself, his major adviser, and the people he has been working with most intensively in his earlier contacts.

8. Cumulative records should be kept by persons concerned with all of the student's experiences.

9. It is desirable for student teachers to have additional experiences while student teaching.

10. The first student teaching experience should be in the best school available. Additional student teaching experiences should be in typical situations. It is important for the student to be thinking of how to move from the quality of the school he is in to the better situation.

11. It is desirable that the student while student teaching carry one course that is focused on problems related to student teaching.

12. Student teaching experiences should be planned and carried out as an integral part of the total teacher education program. All persons concerned in the student teaching experience should participate in planning the experience.

13. A period of concentrated full-time student teaching should be provided for all students.

14. Adjustments should be made within the student teaching experience to meet the needs of individual students.

15. The student teacher and cooperating teacher should teach cooperatively from the very first day that the student teacher is in the classroom. The student teacher and cooperating teacher should plan and share together, so that the student is a part of the on-going activity.

16. The student teaching experience should include, as nearly as possible, the full experience of the in-service teacher.

17. The student teacher should be assisted in understanding children and in establishing a set of operating principles.

18. Only the student and the cooperating teacher can determine when the student shall take over the full responsibility of teaching. This should be when the student, himself, is ready.

19. Observation and participation should be continued throughout the student teaching experience.

20. The cooperating teacher should have the major responsibility for the supervision of the student teacher.

21. How often the college faculty members, subject matter as well as professional, visit the student should depend upon the needs of the student and the needs of the cooperating teacher as to supervision.

22. Assignment to student teaching should be a cooperative affair, involving the student, the college advisers, and the cooperating teacher or his representative.

A student teaching program, based on the needs and interests of the student, should be functional in the student's experience as a teacher and as a learner. All of the responsibilities of the teacher in practical situations should be included. Wide and varied experiences aid in the development of the future teacher not only as a competent teacher but as a responsible citizen in the community and as an integrated individual. The purpose and principles of student teaching go beyond the preparation and need for the classroom and take into account the prospective teacher's life in the community as well as his optimum growth as an individual.

JAMES B. MacDONALD

ESTHER ZARET

Student Teaching: Benefit or Burden?

Is student teaching a crucial part of a teacher education program? The results of a recent study at the University of Wisconsin-Milwaukee cast doubt on this assumption.[1] The major hypothesis of the study dealt with the observable effects of a research-oriented, student-teaching experience on the improvement of decision-making and problem-solving behavior in teaching. Two assumptions of value provided the central focus: the first, that a systematic, logical, reflective approach to decision making is extremely important to effective teaching; the second, that the student-teaching experience represents a critical ingredient in the preparation of teachers.

A selected group of elementary school student teachers was given systematic

1. Macdonald, James B., and others. *A Research Oriented Elementary Education Student Teaching Program*. U.S. Department of Health, Education, and Welfare, Cooperative Research Project No. 1091. Milwaukee: University of Wisconsin-Milwaukee, 1965.

Dr. Macdonald is professor of education, University of Wisconsin—Milwaukee. Dr. Zaret is assistant professor of education, Marquette University, Milwaukee, Wisconsin.

opportunities to identify individual problems and concerns in a series of interviews planned as one of a comprehensive group of criterion measures. The objective data gathered in the overall study, and the tremendous impact of the personal feelings expressed by the student teachers in the interviews, impressed the investigators with the need to reexamine a basic premise of the entire study—the traditionally held value of the student-teaching experience.

Two groups of above-average students were selected from the total population of elementary education student teachers at the University of Wisconsin-Milwaukee in two successive years.[2] Each student was then randomly assigned to one of three subgroups: the experimental, which received a modified program and research experiences in student teaching; the experimental-control, which received a modified program only; and the control, which experienced no modifica-

2. Selection criterion was a combined standard score derived from three assessments: (1) grade point average (G.P.A.) in first three years of college work, (2) college qualification test (CQT), (3) university instructor's predictive rating of potential teaching success.

JOURNAL OF TEACHER EDUCATION (AACTE), 1971. Vol. 22, pp. 51-58.

tions in program. Measures of knowledge, attitudes, values, ability, personality and performance relevant to teaching and to other more general areas were collected during the semester for all groups, and three interviews were given concerning problems in student teaching. Follow-up performance ratings and interviews were conducted at the end of the first year of teaching. There was a total of sixty-six subjects: twenty-two in each of three groups during two successive years of student teaching, and forty in the combined group available for the follow-up study.[3]

Two kinds of data collected in the context of the larger study are relevant to the question raised here about student teaching: (1) interview data concerning the problems students were encountering in student teaching, and (2) performance predictions and ratings before and during student teaching.

Interview Data

A series of four interviews was planned for each student teacher participating in the study, the first three scheduled at spaced intervals during the student-teaching semester, and the fourth as part of the follow-up program at the end of the first year of classroom teaching. A crucial aspect of the interviewing procedure was a nonthreatening climate to promote free responses without fear of evaluation. It was possible to set up a nonevaluative situation in which the interviewer was not connected with the elementary education teaching program or with the evaluative aspects of the research study. One interviewer conducted the series of interviews for both phases of the study.

The first two interviews, held after the third and twelfth weeks of the student-teaching semester, were focused only on

eliciting statements of problems the students were encountering in student teaching. No attempt was made to structure questions other than to ask students to talk about difficulties they were having and to encourage further student talk by the use of clarifying techniques, such as repeating to the student what he had said to the interviewer or rephrasing his statements in the form of questions. The basic intent was simply to keep him talking about his student-teaching problems until the interviewer sensed that the interview would no longer be productive. The length of the interviews varied, but the average session lasted about forty minutes.

Interview three, semistructured, asked the student teacher to anticipate the kinds of problems he expected to meet in his first year of classroom teaching:

1. On the basis of your student-teaching experience, what concerns or problems do you anticipate in your first year of teaching?
2. What kinds of help will you need to resolve the problem?
3. What possible solutions do you see in the area of your concern?

The fourth interview, which was planned as part of the follow-up program at the end of the first year of classroom teaching, necessarily involved only those students who were doing their first-year teaching in the Milwaukee area. The student was asked to respond to five questions.[4]

1. What have been your major concerns in your first year of teaching?
2. What have you done about them, and in what ways have you attempted to resolve them?
3. Have you tried any new ideas in your

---

3. Macdonald, James B., and others, *op. cit.*

4. The third interviews for student teachers who were not available for the follow-up program are not included in the analysis for this study.

classroom that you had not anticipated using?

4. What kind of self-improvement activities have you participated in during this last year?

5. In what ways could our teacher education program have better prepared you for your teaching job?[5]

Content analysis of the interviews. The interviews were analyzed through a content analysis system devised to identify and categorize the student's frame of reference or primary orientation for each concern he specified. The three general categories of analysis were (a) classroom-learning orientation, (b) student-teacher orientation, and (c) no problems, 1 and 2. The major categories were subdivided into thirteen problem areas. A problem focus relating primarily to classroom teaching and learning was considered a more objective orientation than that relating primarily to the position of student teaching.

Analysis of the interview data. The data gathered in the series of interviews were analyzed in answer to three questions, each of which will be considered in turn:

1. *Are there significant differences between the experimental and the control groups in the kinds of problems identified and described?* This question grew out of the hunch that the students who participated in the research-oriented student-teaching program would become more objectively oriented to problems in student teaching. The data collected by interviews were examined to see whether or not a notable shift toward objectivity took place during the first two months of the experimental program (i.e., between the first and second interviews).

A chi square test was run for the first

and second interviews for all three groups to examine the proportion of responses in classroom-centered or objective categories versus student-teacher-centered or personal categories. A two-problem by three-group table resulted for each interview. No significant differences between groups (.05) were found in either interview one or two. Inspection of proportions revealed a slight shift toward nonobjective problems for all groups. Thus, the experimental group did not become more objective in its problem statement. A chance finding of some interest was the high proportion of identified problems that were related to a student-teaching situation: the majority of problems verbalized during both interviews can be classified as having been created by the student-teaching situation.

2. *Are there significant differences between groups in the degree of realistic predictions of problems made for the first year of teaching?* Problems predicted in the third interview were analyzed by groups and then compared with the actual problems identified in the follow-up interviews. The discrepancy between what was predicted and what actually became a problem was expressed in the percentage of problems identified in the third interview that did not appear in the fourth. In Table 1, a lower percentage indicated

5. Analysis of responses to questions 4 and 5 are not included in this report.

TABLE 1

Group	Percentage of problems Identified in Third Interview Not Appearing in Fourth Interview
Experimental	37 percent
Experimental-Control	43 percent
Control	55 percent

direction toward a more accurate or realistic prediction.

These results suggest a possibility of more realistic predictions on the part of the experimental and experimental-control groups, with the direction of differences suggesting that the research-oriented group was most realistic.

3. *Are there significant differences between groups in the range and application of alternative solutions to problems identified during first-year teaching?* An analysis was made of the range of utilization of alternative solution processes during the first year of teaching. Seven categories of solutions were developed from the data:

(a) Use of research method, including collecting of data
(b) Study method, including formal classes or informal learnings, e.g., readings
(c) Trial and error
(d) Insight
(e) Attempts to apply previously learned solutions
(f) Clinics and observations in other classrooms
(g) Seeking help from school personnel

Of these seven categories, two were markedly typical of the experimental group only. The use of research (five responses) and of observation in others' classrooms (five responses) was unique to the research group, with the exception of one response for observation in the control group. This appeared to be a notable extension in the range of solutions employed by the experimental group in comparison with the other two groups.

The seven categories were combined into four for analysis by the chi square test. The chi square obtained did not meet the .05 criterion level for sig-

nificance; consequently, there were considered to be no statistically significant differences among the three groups in the relative proportion of the kinds of alternative solutions utilized during the first year of teaching. The only noticeable difference, not large enough to produce a statistically significant difference, was the total absence of use of the research process in any group but the experimental.

Summary of findings from interview data. No statistically significant differences were found in the hypothesized areas of change. The series of interviews did yield some puzzling phenomena and some intriguing hunches that were not readily amenable to the planned quantitative analysis (nor perhaps to any formal analysis). The most relevant of these data have been sorted into two areas for further study.

1. The first set of phenomena is related to the limitations and the positive aspects of the interview techniques as used in this study. There was some evidence of hostility and resistance in the early interviews and some real concern expressed in response to the interviewing methods, but as students became freer and more accepting of the nonevaluative situation, they tended to see the interviews as gripe sessions and made use of the situation to unburden themselves of a wide range of nonobjective problems. Unintentionally, then, the freedom of the interview situation may have served in varying degrees as release for some students and thus may have obscured the quantitative findings of the study. On the positive side, the freedom of the interview situation served to define differences in the readiness of individuals to profit by the research-

oriented program or by any other kind of student-teaching program.

In the free discussion of problems, concerns, and interests related to student-teaching experiences, some students seemed strikingly more open to change than did others. The hunch concerning openness as a dimension of effectiveness in teaching has been investigated in another study.[6]

2. The second set of phenomena is related to the disparity—almost a dichotomy—in the behavior of the student teachers as compared with their subsequent behavior as first-year teachers. The differences were especially evident in reaction to the interviews and in orientation to problems. There was a marked contrast between the resistance to the early interviews during student teaching and the positive response to the follow-up interviews, held on a voluntary basis for students doing their first year of classroom teaching in the Milwaukee area. These interviews were held on Saturdays or during spring vacation; yet, all but two teachers of the group available responded with interest, cooperation, and a generally more objective orientation to classroom problems.

The disparity noted in student teacher—first-year teacher behavior suggests the continuing orientation of the student teacher as student rather than as teacher, with an abrupt change in identification occurring some time during the first year of teaching.

An immediate question is raised by our experience with the interviews: How uni-

versal are the problems and concerns identified by this group of student teachers? Findings in this study regarding teaching performance sharply underline the growing concern about the validity of the assumption that the student-teaching experience is a necessary and beneficial element in the preservice preparation of teachers. If, as traditionally conceived, it does give rise to such universal and frustrating problems for student teachers, perhaps alternative methods should be devised for inducting students into the teaching profession with more finesse and less trauma.

Performance Predictions and Ratings

1. The *instructors' predictive rating of success in teaching* was one of a group of selection measures included here because of its unexpected and highly significant relatedness to both sets of on-the-job performance ratings described below. The predictive rating of potential success in teaching was made after nine weeks of student teaching by the university instructor responsible for the preexperimental group to which the student had been regularly assigned.

2. *Performance of teachers in the instructional setting* during student teaching and first-year teaching was one of three basic categories of criterion variables in the study. The performance variables were measured by trained observers using the following instruments and/or techniques:

Student teaching:	Ryans' *Teacher Characteristics Study Observation Scale*—(1) summary rating by cooperating teacher, (2) summary rating by university supervisor, (3) observer rating for one visit
First-year teaching:	(1) Ryans' *Teacher Characteristics Study Observa-*

6. Macdonald, James B., and Zaret, Esther. *A Study of Openness in Classroom Interactions.* U. S. Department of Health, Education, and Welfare, National Institute of Mental Health, No. 07563-01. Milwaukee: University of Wisconsin-Milwaukee, 1967.

tion Scale—three observations by two alternating teams of trained observers, (2) Macdonald-Doll *Conditions for Learning Scale* (revised)—three ratings by two alternating teams of trained raters

Summary of findings on performance prediction and ratings. The three separate ratings during student teaching made by the cooperating teacher, the university supervisor, and a trained observer on the Ryans *Teacher Characteristics Observation Scale* showed the intercorrelations listed in Table 2.

These correlations were accepted as evidence of sufficient reliability on performance rating in student teaching to accept the data as meaningful.

Follow-up ratings during first year teaching. The question of whether the findings of this study are relevant to first-year performance was examined by relating the first-year performance ratings made by observers on 40 of the 66 subjects to the variables assessed by an observer, university supervisor, and a critic teacher during the student-teaching experience.

The summated ratings on the two rating scales used (Ryans' *Teacher Characteristics Observation Scale* and the Macdonald-Doll *Conditions for Learning*

TABLE 2
Correlations of Performance Made by Three Separate Raters During Student Teaching

	Observer	Cooperating Teacher	University Supervisor
Observer	—	.75*	.71*
Cooperating Teacher		—	77*
University Supervisor			—

* Significant at or beyond the .05 level

Scale) correlated .92 when used by the three trained observers who visited each classroom three times. The correlation between first-year ratings and student-teacher ratings are reported in Table 3.

It is apparent that correlations between ratings made during student teaching and those made at the end of the first year of teaching are low; none are significant at the .05 level. Thus, we have a phenomenon of highly correlated intraratings at each period (student teaching and first year) that are not highly interrelated between the two periods of assessment. The follow-up ratings, however, are consistent with ratings made during student teaching, in that the pattern of significant correlations with other variables reveals significant relationships to:

TABLE 3
Performance Correlations Between Raters
Student Teaching and First Year

	S. T. Obs.	S.T.C.T.	S.T.U.S.	Ryans	Macdonald-Doll
Stu. Tchr. Obs.	—	.75*	.71*	.18	.22
Stu. Tchr. C. T.		—	.77*	.12	.17
Stu. Tchr. U. S.			—	.19	.26
Ryans				—	.92*
Macdonald-Doll					—

* Significant at .05 or beyond

(1) The selection criterion of group leader prediction,

(2) The *Minnesota Teacher Attitude Inventory,*

(3) Interest in identification with others, as measured by a subsection of *Manifold Interest Inventory.*

Conclusions

The essentially unrelated nature of the findings of observations during student teaching and of observations at the end of the first year of teaching was a surprising and thought-provoking finding. The correlation on the rating scales between observers in the follow-up study and between rating scales during each separate period are the highest correlations obtained in the study, thus providing evidence of high reliability yet essentially no relationship between periods.

This finding surely suggests that the pressure of actual first-year teaching may produce considerably greater alteration of teacher behavior than that which took place during student teaching. Of course, one might hypothesize that student teacher behavior is essentially a conforming behavior that does not reflect the true action tendencies of the student, but either conclusion casts some doubt on the traditionally held value of student-teaching experience.

The data gathered by the interviews add to this doubt. It was somewhat of a shock to note that over half of the problems students verbalized during student teaching were related purely to the conditions of student teaching. If one assumes that productive learning of desirable teaching behavior is the goal of student teaching, it would seem undesirable to create considerably more problems for students through the nature of the teacher education program rather than finding some way to focus students primarily on classroom learning problems. Bach's [7] finding that there is no relationship between student-teaching ability and success in the field seems congruent with the results reported here.

The only measure that remains significantly related to both sets of performance ratings is the selection measure, the prediction of success in teaching made by university instructors who had observed the students for nine weeks in the beginning phases of student teaching. The fact that these early predictions of success remained significantly correlated to performance at the end of student teaching, and also at the end of the first year of teaching, raises some interesting speculations. By and large, one might say that first impressions are fairly accurate. But perhaps even more to the point, this finding raises questions about change brought about by the student-teaching experience. Why should there be such a high correlation after 27 more weeks of student teaching? What changes have been brought about?

Even more startling are the carry-over findings in the first year of teaching. If ratings after the first year are essentially unrelated to those during student teaching, why should instructor predictions correlate significantly with both sets of data? Are we to assume that a single prediction of success by a qualified instructor after an initial look at a student teacher is the best single index of future performance in teaching?

Part of the answer to these questions may lie in the nature of the program involved. It is important to remember that the particular group experience at University of Wisconsin-Milwaukee involved the instructor in a supervisory experience

7. Bach, Jacob O. "Practice Teaching Success in Relation to Other Measures of Teaching Ability." *Journal of Experimental Education* 21: 57-80; September 1952.

during one-half of each day and a continuous instructional relationship with the same students during the other half. Instructors were able to see and know students in a variety of situations revealing many aspects of performance, cognitive ability, and personality. This global experiencing of students by qualified persons may well provide the best predictive procedure.

The question remains as to why this prediction is possible if the major portion of the student-teaching experience lies ahead, as well as the experience of first-year teaching. Two possible explanations are suggested: (1) that the criteria used for prediction were almost identical to the rating dimensions used for observations; or (2) that there is a global quality about individuals tied to personality and ability but evidenced in interpersonal relations as a gestalt that remains essentially consistent regardless of training method or traditional student-teaching experience.

The second hypothesis seems more plausible to the writers. If this explanation were confirmed in future studies, it would suggest that teacher education programs would be better focused on the quality of persons rather than on a wide variety of performances of individuals. From the experiences in this study, the writers would identify two essential dimensions of an alternative student-teaching experience:

1. Opportunities for free expression of problems and concerns
2. Opportunities for systematic clarification and refocusing of the student's orientation to his problems

Under any circumstance, a basic assumption of this study concerning the significance of the traditionally conceived student-teaching experience should be seriously questioned.

The Teaching Center
Assists in Resource Use

ARNOLD L. WILLEMS
MAX H. BROWN

COLLEGES and universities, public schools, and sometimes state departments of education, in striving for relevant experiences in the preparation of teachers, are being driven toward deeper and deeper complementary relationships. A consortium approach, for example, is causing greater emphasis to be placed on the development of teaching centers.

Diverse functions of teaching centers make definition difficult. Most teaching centers concentrate on student teaching, attempting to provide a higher quality of student teaching experiences. Examples of such centers are the Multi-Institutional Kanawha County Student Teaching Center [1] and the Metro-Atlanta Teacher Education Center.[2] Some teaching centers facilitate programs which correlate methods courses as closely as possible with student teaching, the primary objective being to fuse theory and practice.

[1] Kathryn Maddox. "Multi-Institutional Kanawha County Student Teaching Center." Charleston, West Virginia: Kanawha County Board of Education, 200 Elizabeth Street, n.d. 12 pp.

[2] Charles K. Franzen. "The Metro-Atlanta Teacher Education Center Model." Atlanta: Atlanta Area Teacher Education Service, n.d. 6 pp.

EDUCATIONAL LEADERSHIP, November 1972, pp. 131-133.

Perhaps the greatest impact of these centers is being felt in that educational no man's land, the gap between theory and practice. Methods courses taught on the site concurrently with classroom observations and student teaching help bridge this gap. BRUTEP, a cooperative venture of the State University of New York, College of Brockport, and the City School District of Rochester, New York,[3] is an example of such a center, as are the Wayne State University— Detroit Public Schools Teaching Centers [4] and the Elementary Participation Program of the University of Wyoming and Laramie County School District Number One of Cheyenne, Wyoming.[5]

In any case, the teaching center becomes most meaningful when it functions as the agency responsible for increasing the utilization of all available resources in the teacher education process. Among many advantages, the utilization of indigenous human and physical resources is perhaps the key to the unique success of the teaching center. Effective use of. these resources increases the responsibility and somewhat changes the role of the college supervisor or, in some cases, a resident faculty member who is assigned to the center. This person is often designated as center director.

Certainly the center director's role is extended and made more complex than that

[3] Colden B. Garland and Dorothy E. Foster. "BRUTEP: A Response to Dr. Aspy's 'Maslow and Teachers in Training.'" *The Journal of Teacher Education* 23 (17): 47-49; Spring 1972.

[4] "Wayne State University—Detroit Public Schools Teaching Center Models." Detroit: Wayne State University and Detroit Public Schools, 201 Mackenzie Hall, n.d.

[5] Arnold L. Willems. "Bridging the Gap Between Theory and Practice—The Pilot Participation Program in Cheyenne." *Wyoming Education News* 38 (6): 16-17, 26-27; February 1972.

of the traditional college supervisor. No longer is he merely an observer and evaluator of student teachers. He may teach methods courses. He is involved more than ever with public relations. Most important, his tasks as teaching center director include identification of physical and human resources and planning and coordinating their effective use.

The center director must know the community well. A thorough knowledge of its physical facilities is of great importance. Institutions, both public and private, are potential contributors of needed resources. Museums, industry, state and local public libraries, and welfare agencies can contribute unique and valuable services. For example, state libraries and museums can contribute specialized materials about state and regional history. Welfare agencies can provide information concerning the social background of the schools' children and youth and the relationship of the school to the community.

The public school system may make available for teaching center use its professional library and curriculum materials center, which may include professional books and journals, films, filmstrips, textbooks, kits, games, and various other instructional aids. If the public school system has a television studio, it can be utilized by university students for micro-teaching. Video tapes produced by public school educators and university instructors can be an invaluable aid in methods classes and in-service programs. Public school systems may provide classrooms for student teaching seminars and methods instruction in one or more of their school buildings.

If, as in some cases, the teaching center is a separate entity with its own physical structure containing offices, classrooms, and library, public school and community personnel may avail themselves of these resources. Classrooms can be utilized for seminars, adult education classes, and extension courses. The community may borrow audio-visual equipment, such as video-tape recorders, and use the center's professional library. The use of physical facilities, then, can and should be a two-way street, with both the public and the teaching center gaining mutual benefits. A true sharing of resources enhances the educational experiences of all concerned.

The center director must have a good understanding of the people of the community, including their social, economic, and cultural differences. Effective lines of communication must be developed and maintained with the various agencies which contribute resources. The teaching center concept cannot be imposed upon a public school system and community by the university. It is essential that teachers and administrators, along with community representatives, be involved in cooperative planning.

The teaching center is in the favored position of having available practically unlimited human resources. As succinctly stated by Edward C. Pomeroy:

The way is opening up for the use of new resources to make the education of new teachers more meaningful and more directly associated with the schools, where the action is.[6]

Public school students, classroom teachers, librarians, curriculum specialists, audio-visual coordinators, administrators, and auxiliary personnel are usually happy and willing to share their capabilities in provid-

[6] Edward C. Pomeroy. *Beyond the Upheaval*. Washington, D.C.: American Association of Colleges of Teacher Education, 1972. p. 14.

ing educational experiences for university students. Pupils may be available for micro-teaching and for demonstration lessons. For instance, these lessons may exemplify methods of fostering an inquiring attitude through problem solving and guided discovery.

Increasingly, classroom teachers are being called on to share their expertise, to assist in planning, and to present demonstration lessons. In addition to assisting in methods classes, they may open their classrooms for university students to observe inductive modes of teaching and learning, classroom environments which are pupil oriented rather than teacher oriented, organizational patterns such as open classrooms and schools and individualization of instruction, and the use of interest centers to facilitate the teaching-learning process. The feedback and criticisms of supervising teachers and involved principals can assist the teaching center director in upgrading the quality of the entire program.

Curriculum specialists or resource teachers may assist in making methods instruction practical and down-to-earth. Examples of such practical instruction at the elementary level could be in handwriting, how children learn to spell, creative writing tips, and an introduction to a variety of language arts materials. These specialists may open doors for university students to become involved in workshops, in-service programs, and meetings with publishers' representatives. A hiring official may discuss with university students what they may expect during a job interview and what the interviewer may consider as crucial factors for employment.

State departments of education and professional education associations may contribute additional specialized personnel. Certification requirements may be presented and justified by the state department, while education associations may present information on the professionalization of teachers. These organizations may also serve as invaluable sources for program feedback and interpretation of the various aspects of the teaching center's operation to their wider memberships. One way this can be accomplished is through their publications.

The teaching center should reciprocate by serving as a clearinghouse for university information. Information about enrollment, transfer of credit, correspondence courses, extension classes, and adult education programs may be readily available. The teaching center may also provide university catalogs, class schedules, and calendars of university events.

Teaching center personnel may serve as off-campus advisors in helping students plan their programs of study. They may develop in-service programs and serve as consultants for the public school system. Again emphasis must be placed on cooperative planning, which allows all agencies involved to realize the potential uses of the vast array of human resources.

Moving Toward Reality

The concept of the teaching center improves teacher education through a more systematic identification, categorization, and utilization of the resources existing within an educational community. This enables teaching center programs to:

1. Move toward the fusion of theory and practice in methods courses and student teaching

2. Through a mutual sharing of resources, strengthen the bond of cooperation between

public schools, colleges and universities, and the community

    3. Allow input of public school people into teacher preparation programs

    4. Encourage professors of education to change their orientation from the university setting to the real world of the public school classroom.

The teaching center is an emerging institution offering great promise for improvement in the education of teachers. It brings the university to the practitioner and the practitioner to the university. By bringing these two together, the teaching center makes more effective and beneficial use of the many resources available. This pooling of resources for the education of teachers is a move toward reality. The resources of colleges and universities, public school systems, and the community become the process and the crucible for teacher education.

Geraldine Murphy

The Prospective Teacher
as Observer

A scheme for observing is needed to guide the prospective teacher before, during, and after observation of teaching.

NEITHER an onlooker nor a spectator is, properly speaking, an observer. For observing involves careful consideration of a certain fact or event; it implies close and directed attention.

Anyone who, uninitiated, has viewed a surgical operation, looked through a microscope, or watched a ball game knows that looking becomes observing only when a framework defines what is to be looked at and a focus directs the viewer's attention in certain ways to selected aspects of the event.

The spectator's need for precise guidance increases if the event being watched involves such complicating factors as a number of persons, continuous movement, or any kind of constant change. As the chances for confusion are multiplied, so is the novice's need for ways of ordering the experience.

He must be "told what to watch for." He must be made aware of what the "classic situations" are, what moves may be expected, and what "rules" guide the performance. He must be shown where to concentrate his attention so that the sequences of cause, act, and

effect that constitute the particular event he is viewing will become clear and meaningful to him. He will "see" the performance only by knowing what to look at and how to look at it.

If the novice anticipates becoming more than just an intelligent observer, if he intends to engage in the occupation—to *be* a surgeon, a biologist, or a ballplayer—then what he observes and the way he observes it should be altered accordingly. Participation in a field entails performance, and the prospective participant needs to observe whatever activities he will have to be able to perform when he enters his chosen field of work.

These activities can be specified by ascertaining, for example, what skills would be expected of him, what competence in these skills consists of, what obstacles he might encounter, what constitutes achieving goals in the particular occupation. Answers to inquiries such as these would indicate the exact types of performances it would be most useful and pertinent for a future participant to look at.

JOURNAL OF TEACHER EDUCATION (AACTE), 1962. Vol. 13, pp. 150-156.

His manner and mode of observing should also differ from that of a mere informed spectator. The prospective participant needs to observe the performances of these relevant skills analytically, evaluatively, and creatively.

Observation for those preparing to participate in an occupation should be arranged and directed, first, to afford opportunities for a detailed, critical analysis of competent "live" performance of the skill or skills the occupation involves; secondly, to stimulate a continual evaluation of the various parts of the performance as well as of the whole; and thirdly, to encourage a vicarious role-playing, in which the novice tries to "improve" the performance he observes by changes he devises and "tries out" in his imagination.

This kind of observation fosters the habit of studying the factors in a situation carefully and inclusively; it urges the development of a set of critical principles by which to evaluate and improve performances; it promotes a systematically critical attitude, which the novice can later assume toward his own performances.

Observation of Teaching

Candidates in teaching programs are prospective participants in a field, and what they look at during the classroom observations and how they look at it should be arranged accordingly. The novice "teacher" ought not to be merely a casual onlooker or an uninitiated spectator in a classroom.

The period of observing, which generally precedes actual practice, is an important interim in teacher education. The prospective teacher has then his only opportunity, before actually facing a class, to translate his theoretical understanding of the teaching of subject matter into a practical understanding of what is usable in particular, "live" classes, where twenty or more learners are involved in constantly changing circumstances.

During this period the novice can confront without threat or anxiety the often undreamed-of problems of bringing "live" students to a living subject matter and can deal with his dilemmas calmly and thoughtfully "at the back of the room."

The period of observation is, then, a necessary buffer zone between the study of educational theory and actual teaching. In order to make proper and full use of his period of watching in the classroom, the prospective teacher must be apprised of what the crucial aspects of teaching a lesson are, so that he will know what to focus his attention upon.

He must be guided as to how to examine, in precise ways and for reasons he understands, these aspects of a teaching performance. He must be directed as to how to assess by objective standards the performance he observes. And he must be urged to recommend changes which, on the basis of his analysis and evaluation, he would try to effect. Briefly, the prospective teacher must learn how to analyze, evaluate, and "improve" the total class situation he is observing.

A Scheme for Observing

The following pages offer a scheme in question form designed to guide prospective teachers in their analysis, evaluation, and "improvement" of the teaching of a lesson.

The scheme is divided into five parts, each one representing an important aspect of a teaching performance: (1) The Objective, (2) The Subject Matter, (3) The Teaching Techniques, (4) The Design of the Lesson, and (5) The Close. Each part is subdivided to suggest some of the chief constituents of the aspect that the observer should analyze and evaluate separately and interrelatedly.

The questions under these subdivisions are grouped to assist him in his probings and judgments. At the end of each of the five parts there is a special section, "Improving the Performance," that invites the observer to make his own proposals for bettering the exercise of that particular teaching skill in the particular class being observed.

The observer can use the scheme in its entirety for the critical observation of a complete class lesson. But since each of the five parts concentrates on a certain aspect of a teaching performance, each can be used independently or in conjunction with one or more of the others. The scheme lends itself to any order or pattern of organization that suits the need or the interest of the user.

It seems unlikely, however, that a novice could profitably use the entire scheme during any of his early observations. He would perhaps find it more productive to devote one or more observations to each one of the five aspects in turn and then to attempt to interrelate the five during subsequent observations.

The scheme can be used to guide the prospective teacher before, after, or during observation. He might study the entire scheme in detail before he begins to observe so that he can develop an initial framework by which to examine a lesson. Or he might use the scheme as a guide for a "post-mortem" of any lesson he observes. Or when the appropriate grammatical changes are made in the scheme, the novice might use it during the observation to ask himself questions about the performance going on before him. And although the set of questions was designed primarily for observing, it is also a suitable instrument for apprentice teachers, interns, beginning teachers—and supervisors of student teaching—to use in the analysis, criticism, and evaluation of teaching performances.

The Scheme

I. *The Objective*
A. Making the Objective Clear

1. How soon after the start of the class period did the objective for the lesson become clear to you? By what means did it become clear?

2. How soon did the objective become clear to the students? How did you know it was clear to them? For instance, what behavioral changes did you notice? Was there a marked change in their involvement? a lessening in bewilderment?

3. What means was used to make the objective clear? For example, was the class told the objective explicitly:

   a. by the teacher's saying, "Yesterday, we did X, so today we shall . . ."?

   b. by a topic for the day or an outline of some sort on the board that told or suggested "what we are doing and why"?

   c. by the teacher's distinguishing frankly between "what we are trying to do and what we are not trying to do"—a distinction often necessary if the class is slow or if the natural associations of the material at hand tend to draw in irrelevancies?

4. Was the over-all objective purposely withheld? Was the class given only a sequence of "hints" (mediate objectives) for each step in their work? Why? Was the work new? difficult? Would you have judged the class psychologically ready to know the objective from the outset? On what are you basing your judgment?

5. To what extent did the previous assignment reveal what the objective for the day would be?

B. Keeping the Objective Clear

1. Did the objective remain clear throughout the lesson? For example, did every question that the teacher asked lead definitely toward accomplishing the objective? Did every response that the teacher rewarded

contribute in some recognizable and defensible way toward achieving the goal?

2. Could you have stated at any particular moment exactly where the class was in relation to achieving the objective?

3. Did the class know at all times what it was trying to achieve? Or had some "lost track"?

   a. How did you know they had lost track: by inattention? random answers? guessing? anxieties?

   b. Why had they lost track? (1) Did the teacher fail to interrelate the questions? (2) Were syntheses too infrequent? (3) Were tangential responses or questions or remarks "honored"? (4) Did the teacher change the level of questioning without preparing the class; that is, without requiring the students responding at the more sophisticated level to tell the class how they arrived at their answers?

C. Improving the Performance

If you were to teach the subject matter of this lesson to this group of students:

1. What objective would you choose?

2. What means other than those used could be employed to define the area of the lesson and to make known its purpose and its approximate structure?

3. How specifically would you make the objective clear to these students?

4. What might frustrate your attempts to keep your objective clear to this class throughout an entire lesson?

5. How would you anticipate these potential blocks?

II. *The Subject Matter and the Materials*

A. Appropriateness of the Subject Matter and of the Viewpoint on It

1. What segment of the subject matter was being studied? For example, if the subject matter was chemistry, was the segment "oxygen"? if history, was it "the Civil War"? if English, was it "Irving"?

2. Is that segment of the subject matter the most appropriate that could be selected, the objective, the subject matter, and the class being what they are? On what are you basing your judgment?

3. From what viewpoint or with what focus was the particular segment of subject matter being studied? For example, if the segment was the Civil War, was the focus "the campaigns of the Civil War," or "the causes of the Civil War," or "the social consequences of internal war"?

4. Considering the objective, the subject matter, and the class, in what ways would you say that the viewpoint or the focus was suitable or unsuitable?

5. What exactly are the other segments of the subject matter or other viewpoints on it that would have been

   a. more pertinent to the objective?

   b. more central to the subject matter?

   c. more significant for this class?

6. In what ways precisely is each suggestion you have made more pertinent, or more central, or more significant?

7. Are there any segments or any approaches that are eminently suitable to the objective *and* to the subject matter *and* to the class? On what precisely are you basing your judgment about this threefold appropriateness?

B. Appropriateness of Presentation

If the lesson seemed inappropriate, was it the subject matter or the viewpoint on it that was unsuitable or was it *really* the manner of presentation that was unfit? An example may clarify this important difference. Let us say that the subject matter was English grammar; the segment, adjectives; and the focus, modification. If the lesson seemed inappropriate, was it so because the adjective was an improper segment of subject matter to be studied? or because modification was an unsuitable focus? Or rather:

1. Was the manner of presentation subverting the objective? For example, if the objective was "to teach students to use subordinating constructions for modifying ideas," was the teacher mistakenly concentrating on defining or analyzing adjective constructions?

2. Did the teacher's manner of presentation show that he was unmindful that as a subject matter grammar is studied only as a means to and an explanation of expressive composition?

3. Was the manner of presentation unsuitable for the class? Did the teacher, insensitive to the level of the class, dwell on the concept of adjectival modification in a most theoretical way?

C. Appropriateness of Materials

1. Were the materials being used—the texts, maps, demonstrations, and such—truly suitable to the objective, to the segment of the subject matter studied, to the viewpoint taken, and to the class?

2. What materials should have been omitted? What additional materials were needed? What should have been radically rearranged?

3. If the materials seemed inappropriate, was it really the materials that were unsuitable or the way in which they were being used? For example,

a. If a single text was being used, was it being used mechanically as the basis for mere repetitive drill, rather than imaginatively as a springboard for raising useful questions?

b. If several types of materials—texts, workbooks, dittoed sheets, maps—were being used, (1) did the arrangement of these materials duly economize the learners' time and effort? (2) did the arrangement focus the students' attention on the subject matter or did it distract it to the materials themselves?

D. Improving the Performance

If you were to use your own objective for this lesson:

1. What specific segment of subject matter and what viewpoint on it would you choose?

2. How would you justify your selection in terms of your objective, the subject matter as a whole, and the class you are observing?

3. What materials would you choose? Why those?

4. Specifically in what ways would you use them? Why?

III. *The Techniques*

A. Establishing a Context

1. How was the learning situation "set up"? How, for example, was the lesson opened?

2. How was it explicitly related to the previous lesson, or lessons, or to some other larger whole? In other words, how did the teacher show that he was aware of the kinds of things students would have to know before they could do whatever the lesson would require?

B. Motivating

1. What techniques were used to arouse students' interest in the subject matter?

2. Were these techniques really appropriate to the objective as the teacher seemed to interpret it? as you would interpret it?

3. Were these techniques valid in terms of the subject matter?

a. Or did they distort it; for example, present history as fiction or literature as psychology?

b. Were the connections that were suggested between the subject matter and the students' "world" devised?

c. Were the connections really extrinsic to the subject matter?

d. Did they disguise unrecognizably what the real connections are? On what are you basing your judgment?

4. Were the techniques used appropriate to the particular class?

a. Or did the teacher underestimate the level of maturity?

b. Or was the teacher using some "ready-made" motivation unsuited to this group?

C. Skill in Choosing Teaching Techniques

1. Were the teaching techniques appropriate to the objective? If, for example, the objective was "to understand . . . ," were the techniques conducive to developing understanding?

2. Were the teaching techniques appropriate to the subject matter being studied?

a. Was what was being discussed discussable? or was it a matter of established fact? or a question for analysis?

b. Should what was being talked about have been demonstrated instead?

c. Should what was being questioned on have been merely read aloud expressively?

3. Were the teaching techniques appropriate to the particular class? For instance, did they subserve the subject matter? or did they confuse these students about which was the end, which the means?

D. Skill in Using Teaching Techniques

1. Was discussion really discussion? Or was each student merely reciting to the teacher or simply remarking about the topic?

2. Was the statement of each question clear and properly directive? That is, did it point out that in order to answer the ques-

tion one must recall facts, or establish causal connections, or weigh alternatives—or carry out some equally specific action or actions?

3. Was the questioning developmental and skillfully manipulated?

4. Were tangents and irrelevancies in lines of discussion or in students' questions dismissed? How? by the class? by the teacher's restating the original question?

5. How soon did you realize that the tangents were tangential?

6. Were complex things made simple? How?

7. Were examples used pertinently? Did they really clarify?

a. Or did the type they were or the way they were used cause them to compete for attention with the idea they were supposed to clarify?

b. How many different areas of experience did the teacher draw examples from?

E. Improving the Performance

1. If you were to bring this class to this portion of the subject matter, what intrinsic motivations would you use?

2. If you had been conducting this lesson:

a. On what grounds would you have distinguished among the pertinent, the relevant, the tangential, and the irrelevant in student responses?

b. How would you have incorporated the first two and maybe three, and how would you have dismissed the fourth?

c. What example, analogy, or explanation would you have used to clarify some particular confusion you noted?

IV. *The Design of the Lesson*

A. The Shape

1. What was the shape or movement of the lesson? For example, was it diagonal (rising in a climactic order)? Or radial (diverging from a center or converging at one)? Or spiral?

2. Was it, in your opinion, the appropriate shape? On what are you basing your judgment?

B. Creating and Maintaining Productive Tension

1. Was there a tension between the students and the subject matter?

2. How specifically was it created?

3. If such tension was not present, why not?

4. If an initial tension was created, how was it maintained?

5. If tension waned, was the decline caused by:

a. the teacher's inability to gauge the attention span of the class?

b. his failure to insist on total involvement?

c. his incompetence in using productively the involvement he achieved?

d. an insensitivity to the class' "signaling" that it was ready to move to a more complex level?

e. an inability to reshape the planned questions "in other words"?

f. an incapacity to bring a continual newness to a topic demanding concentrated study?

C. Improving the Performance

If you had been shaping this lesson:

1. How would you have designed it? Why?

2. How would you have dealt with the problems of maintaining tension that the shape of your lesson would have introduced?

V. *The Close*

A. Concluding the Lesson

1. How was the lesson drawn together at the close: by summary? by synthesis? by the natural evolution of a climax?

2. Was the summary or the stated conclusion or the synthesis really what was in fact reached by the class during the lesson?

B. Extending the Lesson

1. What relation did the assignment have to the lesson?

a. Was it remedial; that is, designed to correct weaknesses revealed by the lesson?

b. Was it intensifying; that is, designed to "fix" what was learned, through new work of a similar level of difficulty?

c. Was it amplifying; that is, designed to give breadth and depth to what was learned, through new work on a more sophisticated level?

2. In view of where the class was at the conclusion of the lesson, did the assignment extend the lesson in an appropriate way? On what are you basing your judgment?

C. Improving the Performance

If you had been conducting this lesson:

1. How would you have closed it?

2. What specific assignment would you have considered most useful? Why?

IN conclusion, two points deserve mention. First, in this scheme it is assumed that teaching in a classroom is trying to get a certain group of students to learn a particular subject matter. Teaching is an attempt to bring them to the subject matter in such a way that it will become part of what each student knows, that is, part of his fund of information, skills, and attitudes. The view that teaching is an attempt to bring students to a subject matter, not the reverse, affects this scheme pervasively. So the word "appropriate"—whether it is applied to materials, mode of presentation, motivating techniques, or whatever—means "valid in terms of the subject matter" and "feasible in terms of the students." The questions throughout this scheme ask the observer to notice how far the teacher's attempt to bring students to the particular subject matter is both "valid" and "feasible."

Secondly, the scheme does not pretend to include all ramifications of each of the five aspects, or all possible subdivisions of each section, or all potential questions. Some of the aspects might be telescoped; the subdivisions within each of the five sections might be reduced in number, regrouped, or increased; the questions might be greatly amplified. In this sense, the scheme is tentative and flexible. But in another sense, the scheme is more definite. It intends to suggest that observers should be examining a teaching performance, that a teaching performance involves certain key skills, and observers should be studying carefully and precisely the exercise of these skills. On one hand, then, the scheme does not purport to be exhaustive, but on the other, it does intend to point out the kinds of questions a prospective teacher should ask about a teaching performance.

TIPS FOR A NEOPHYTE ELEMENTARY TEACHER— BEGINNING A SCHOOL YEAR

F. C. Ellenburg

Each year, many beginning elementary school teachers find themselves faced with that first day of school without really knowing what to do. Experienced teachers know that the first day is a crucial experience for the beginning teacher; it can get the year off to a good start.

Georgia Southern College requested all elementary teachers who participated in the student teaching program to send descriptions of activities they use on that first day of school. The suggestions described herein resulted from the responses of the approximately forty teachers who replied.

Becoming Familiar with School Facilities and Routine

1. Obtain a copy of the school handbook and read it.
2. Become familiar with the cumulative records of your students.
3. Become familiar with your textbooks.
4. Locate the:
   - a. library
   - b. clinic
   - c. offices
   - d. supply center
   - e. fire exits
   - f. record files
   - g. special rooms
   - h. bathrooms
   - i. lunchroom

5. Become acquainted with these personnel and understand their roles:
   - a. janitor
   - b. librarian
   - c. lunchroom workers
   - d. special teachers
   - e. secretary
   - f. supervisors
   - g. principal
   - h. superintendent
   - i. curriculum director
   - j. visiting teacher
   - k. school nurse
   - l. welfare workers
   - m. counselor

THE TEACHER EDUCATOR, Winter 1971-72, pp. 32-35.

6. One needs to understand the procedure for conducting many routine activities. Inquire regarding:

a.	fire drills	i.	accident reporting
b.	extra duty schedule	j.	teachers' meetings
c.	recess duty	k.	receiving textbooks and
d.	bus duty		supplies
e.	chapel or assembly	l.	securing community resources
	schedule	m.	secretarial assistance process
f.	special teachers'	n.	ordering films
	schedules	o.	field trip regulations
g.	library schedule	p.	class parties
h.	PTA meetings		

Helping Students Adjust to School—Primary Grades

1. From the entrance to the school and all along the hall, place life-sized pictures of children, animals and sea life pictures illustrating stories found in children's books. A guide can go along with the children and explain the stories being illustrated. This can help the children break away from mother. They often laugh and become involved in the stories.

2. The first day is not too soon to plan behavior charts. Discuss good listening, getting permission to talk, waiting for one's turn, etc. Children who have a part in setting up rules offer better cooperation in carrying them out. The teacher should talk with the children and let them know what he expects of them and what they may expect of school.

3. Prepare large cut-outs of boys and girls from newsprint. Let each child draw in the features and clothes to make the paper figure look like himself.

4. Teach an action song to get them involved.

5. Have each pupil make a picture of his house. Write his name and address. Use the bulletin board as a map to arrange the houses on streets.

6. Teach finger plays and counting rhymes.

7. Tell a story such as "The Gingerbread Boy" and use the chalkboard to draw one. This stimulates listening and gives a point of focus.

8. At the end of the day, for kindergarteners and first graders, on the garment of each child pin a card with necessary information, such as, name, parent's name, address, bus number.

9. Place on a table, or attach to a wall, a piece of "butcher's" paper, perhaps six to nine feet long. Have crayons available so each child may make a picture of his own choosing.

10. Give each child a sheet of manilla drawing paper. Have him draw a picture of himself and cut it out. Put the pictures on the bulletin board. Write each name on a small piece of paper and attach it under the respective picture. A good caption might be "Here We Are."

11. Idea No. 10 can be used and displayed in a different way. Divide the board into two sections. On the left side, place all the boys' pictures and names; on the right side, do the same for the girls. Captions might be "We Are The Boys" or "We Are The Girls."

12. It is a good idea to display on the bulletin board the various materials the children will be using during the year: scissors, crayons, containers of paste, containers of paint, brushes, pencils, and the like. A caption could be "We Will Be Using These."

13. Set up various interest centers, one in which children might use modeling clay, one in which they might work puzzles, or one for looking at books.

14. Display pictures of some of the familiar nursery rhymes. This will give the class something to talk about. It may help bring a shy child into the conversation.

15. A mother could be asked to come on the first day of school to assist. She might collect fees, insurance money, and lunch money.

16. Get acquainted. Call students' names. Perhaps set this to music.

17. Take a tour of your school building.

18. Summarize the day. Let them tell you how they feel about their first day.

19. Play "mailman." Children sit in a circle. The mailman takes a letter or package (prepared beforehand by the teacher), to the child whose name has been called by the teacher. This child then becomes the new mailman. This is a good way for the children to learn each other's names. It helps the teacher in this regard, too.

20. Children stand when the teacher names the color of some piece of clothing they are wearing. Let each child relate the color to the item he is wearing.

21. Take a tour of the room. Explain how to use all of the facilities.

22. Play "get acquainted" games.

23. To encourage children to learn their telephone numbers and addresses, print this information on a balloon, inflate it, and put

47

it up in the room. At the end of the day, let each child select the balloon with his information.

24. Print the names of the children on cards and arrange them according to birthdays. Pictures representing the different months can be placed around the room. Under these pictures, the appropriate birthday cards can be grouped.

25. Traffic safety is especially important in the beginning of the year. Make the floor of the room a maze of streets with stop signs, railroad crossings, etc. Discuss safety rules. Children can walk the streets and obey the signals.

Helping Students Adjust to School—Upper Elementary Grades

1. Discuss things that pupils would like to know about each other. After this discussion, give them a few minutes to interview those they do not know. After this interviewing procedure, each student is given an opportunity to introduce one person to the class.

2. For the first few days, invite the students to bring snapshots of their summer activities for an attention-getting bulletin board. It is fun to see what others did with family or friends at home, at the beach, or on the farm. It is a good learning experience, too, for a child to talk about his photo. These photographs could also be springboards for creative writing.

3. On the first day of school let them write a very honest appraisal of that day, perhaps entitled, "My First Impressions of the —— Grade." Encourage them to be honest. The teacher can learn ways to improve the students' first contact with that grade level.

4. Make a large map of the United States. Have each student place his name at a location he visited, or from which he had a visitor. Let each child relate some incidents connected with that experience.

5. Study the records and cumulative sheets of your students. Make a questionnaire of items that appear badly out-of-date. Send the questionnaires home to be completed by parents.

6. While students are attending to administrative details, the teacher can assign small groups to make comments on the tape recorder. Later in the day, the tape can be played back for the entire class. Topics might include: "An Exciting Experience," "A Good Book," "My Hobby."

These are but a few ideas that elementary teachers have been willing to share to help get the year under way. Planning well and planning early should help get one off to a good start on that important first day.

Intent, Action and Feedback: A Preparation for Teaching

NED A. FLANDERS

The Problem

The point is that much of what is learned in education courses is neither conceptualized, quantified, nor taught in a fashion that builds a bridge between theory and practice. Education students are only occasionally part of an exciting, systematic, exploration of the teaching process, most infrequently by the instructor's example. How can we create, in education courses, an active, problem-solving process, a true sense of inquiry, and a systematic search for principles through experimentation? At least one factor favors change and that is the lack of solid evidence that anything we are now teaching is clearly associated with any index of effective teaching, with the possible exception of practice teaching.

A great many factors resist curriculum change in teacher education. Perhaps the most important is that genuine curriculum innovation, to be distinguished from tinkering with content and sequence, would require that existing faculty members, old and new alike, think differently about their subject matter, act differently while teaching, and relate differently to their students. For some this is probably impossible, for all it would be difficult. Yet changes do occur when

JOURNAL OF TEACHER EDUCATION (AACTE), 1963, Vol. 14, pp. 251-260.

enough energy is mobilized and convictions are strongly held.

It is a serious indictment of the profession, however, to hear so many education instructors say that their students will appreciate what they are learning *after* they have had some practical teaching experience. What hurts is the obvious hypocrisy of making this statement and then giving a lecture on the importance of presenting material in such a way that the immediate needs and interests of the pupils are taken into consideration. Such instances reveal a misunderstanding of theory and practice. To be understood, concepts in education must be verified by personal field experiences; in turn, field experiences must be efficiently conceptualized to gain insight. With most present practices, the gorge between theory and practice grows deeper and wider, excavated by the very individuals who are pledged to fill it.

One stumbling block is our inability to describe teaching as a series of acts through time and to establish models of behavior which are appropriate to different kinds of teaching situations. This problem has several dimensions. First, in terms of semantics, we must learn how to define our concepts as part of a theory. We also need to organize these concepts into the fewest number of variables necessary to establish principles and make predictions. Too often we try to teach the largest number of variables; in fact, as many as we can think of for which there is some research evidence. Second, in terms of technology, we must develop procedures for quantifying the qualitative aspects of teaching acts so that our students will have tools for collecting empirical evidence. Third, in terms of philosophy, we must decide whether our education students are going to be told about teaching in lectures and read about it in books or if they are going to discover these things for themselves. This paper will be devoted to these three issues, in reverse order.

A Philosophy of Inquiry

When Nathaniel Cantor (5) published his nine assumptions of orthodox teaching, there was little evidence to support his criticisms. Must pupils be coerced into working on tasks? In what way is the teacher responsible for pupils' acquiring knowledge? Is education a preparation for later life rather than a present, living experience? Is subject matter the same to the learner as it is to the teacher? The last decade has provided more evidence in support of Cantor's criticism than it has in defense of existing practice.

H. H. Anderson and his colleagues (1,2,3,4) first demonstrated that dominative teacher contacts create more compliance and resistance to compliance, that dominative teacher contacts with pupils spread to the pupil-to-pupil contacts even in the absence of the teacher, and that this pattern of teaching creates situations in which pupils are more easily distracted and more dependent on teacher initiative.

Flanders and Havumaki (8) demonstrated that dominative teacher influence was more persuasive in changing pupil opinions but that such shifts of opinion were not stable since inner resistance was so high.

A research team in Provo, Utah (9) believes that patterns of spontaneous teacher action can be identified and that more effective patterns can be distinguished from less effective patterns. The difference is that more dominative patterns are less effective.

Our own eight-year research program which involved the development of interaction analysis as a tool for quantifying patterns of teacher influence lends further support to Cantor. The generalizations to follow are based on all teachers observed in our different research projects. This total is only 147 teach-

51

ers, representing all grade levels, six different school districts in two countries; but these teachers came from the extremes of a distribution involving several thousand teachers. The total bits of information collected by interaction analysis are well in excess of 1,250,000.

The present, average domination of teachers is best expressed as the rule of two-thirds. About two-thirds of the time spent in a classroom, someone is talking. The chances are two out of three that this person is the teacher. When the teacher talks, two-thirds of the time is spent by many expressions of opinion and fact, giving some direction and occasionally criticizing the pupils. The fact that teachers are taking too active a part for effective learning is shown by comparing superior with less effective classrooms. A superior classroom scores above average on constructive attitudes toward the teacher and the classwork. It also scores higher on achievement tests of the content to be learned, adjusted for initial ability. In studies (7) of seventh grade social studies and eighth grade mathematics, it was found that the teachers in superior classrooms spoke only slightly less, say 50 to 60 per cent of the time, but the more directive aspects of their verbal influence went down to 40 to 50 per cent. These teachers were much more flexible in the quality of their influence, sometimes very direct, but on more occasions very indirect.

To describe the classrooms which were below average in constructive pupil attitudes and in content achievement (they are positively correlated), just change the rule of two-thirds to the rule of three-fourths plus.

The foregoing evidence shows that no matter what a prospective teacher hears in an education course, he has, on the average, been exposed to living models of what teaching is and can be that are basically quite directive. After fourteen or so years he is likely to be quite dependent, expecting the instructor to tell him what to do, how to do it, when he is finished, and then tell him how well he did it. Now it is in this general context that we turn to the question of how we can develop a spirit of inquiry with regard to teaching.

Thelen (10) has described a model of personal inquiry, as well as other models, and the question is whether teacher education can or should move toward this model. He describes this model as follows *(ibid.,* p. 89) :

> . . . (personal inquiry) is a process of interaction between the student and his natural and societal environment. In this situation the student will be aware of the process of which he is a part; during this process he will be aware of many choices among ways he might behave; he will make decisions among these ways; he will then act and see what happens; he will review the process and study it with the help of books and other people; he will speculate about it, and draw tentative conclusions from it.

Returning to the education course, the student will be aware of the learning process of *that* classroom, he will confront choices, he will make decisions among the choices, he will act and then evaluate his actions, and then he will try to make some sense out of it with the help of books, the instructor, and his peers. This is a tall order, but who knows, it may be the only route to discovery and independence for the prospective teacher.

Occasionally we hear of exciting learning experiences in which education students attain a sort of intellectual spirit of inquiry. A unit on motivation can begin with an assessment of the motivation patterns of the education students. The same assessment procedures can then be used at other grade levels, permitting comparisons and generalizations. Principles of child growth and development can be discovered by observation and learned more thoroughly, perhaps, than is possible with only lecture and reading. But this is not what is meant by inquiry.

Inquiry in teacher education means translating understanding into action as part of the teaching process. It means experimenting with one's own behavior, obtaining objective information about one's own behavior, evaluating this information in terms of the teacher's role; in short, attaining self-insight while acting like a teacher.

Procedures for obtaining self-insight have been remarkably improved during the last decade in the field of human relations training. Two characteristics of these training methods seem relevant to this discussion. First, information and insights about behavior must become available in a way that can be accepted and in a form that is understood. Second, opportunities to utilize or act out these insights must be provided. Our ability to accept information about ourselves is a complex problem, but it helps if we believe the information is objective, valid, and given in an effort to help rather than hurt. Our understanding of this information will depend a great deal on our ability to organize the information conceptually. Freedom to act at least requires freedom from threat or embarrassment.

From all of these things, a spirit of inquiry develops.

The Technique of Interaction Analysis

Interaction analysis is nothing more and nothing less than an observation technique which can be used to obtain a fairly reliable record of spontaneous verbal statements. Most teacher influence is exerted by verbal statements, and to determine their quality is to approximate total teacher influence. This technique was first developed as a research tool, but every observer we ever hired testified that the process of learning the system and using it in classrooms was more valuable than anything else he learned in his education courses. Since interaction analysis is only a technique, it probably could be applied to teacher education in a fashion that is consistent or even totally inconsistent with a philosophy of personal inquiry. How it is used in teacher preparation is obviously as important as understanding the procedure itself.

The writing of this manuscript followed the completion of a terminal contract report of a U.S. Office of Education-sponsored, inservice training program based on interaction analysis as a tool for gathering information. How we used interaction analysis is illustrated by the conditions we tried to create for the fifty-five participating teachers, most of whom represented about one-half of the faculties of two junior high schools:[1]

1) Teachers developed new (to them) concepts as tools for thinking about their behavior and the consequences of their behavior. These concepts were used to discover principles of teacher influence. Both types of concepts were necessary: those for describing actions and those for describing consequences.

2) Procedures for assessing both types of concepts in practical classroom situations were tried out. These procedures were used to test principles, to modify them, and to determine when they might be appropriately applied.

3) The training activities involved in becoming proficient in the assessment of spontaneous behavior, in and of themselves, increased the sensitivity of teachers to their own behavior and the behavior of others. Most important, teachers could compare their intentions with their actions.

---

[1] Interaction analysis as a research tool has been used ever since R. F. Bales first developed a set of categories for studying groups. Most of our research results can be found in the references at the end of this paper. Its use as a training device is more recent. Projects have taken place in New Jersey, Philadelphia, Chicago, and Minneapolis. Systematic evaluation is available in only the Minneapolis project.

4) By avoiding a discussion of right and wrong ways of teaching and emphasizing the discovery of principles of teacher influence, teachers gradually became more independent and self-directing. Our most successful participants investigated problems of their own choosing, designed their own plans, and arranged collaboration with others when this seemed advantageous.

Five filmstrips and one teacher's manual have been produced and written. These materials would have to be modified before they could be used with undergraduate students. Before asking how interaction analysis might be used in teacher preparation, we turn next to a description of the procedures.

The Procedure of Observation

The observer sits in a classroom in the best position to hear and see the participants. At the end of each three-second period, he decides which category best represents the communication events just completed. He writes this category number down while simultaneously assessing communication in the next period and continues at a rate of 20 to 25 observations per minute, keeping his tempo as steady as possible. His notes are merely a series of numbers written in a column, top to bottom, so that the original sequence of events is preserved. Occasionally marginal notes are used to explain the class formation or any unusual circumstances. When there is a major change in class formation, the communication pattern, or the subject under discussion, a double line is drawn and the time indicated. As soon as the total observation is completed, the observer retires to a nearby room and completes a general description of each separate activity period separated by the double lines, including the nature of the activities, the class formation, and the position of the teacher. The observer also notes any additional facts that seem pertinent to an adequate interpretation and recall of the total visit.

The ten categories that we used for interaction analysis are shown in Table 1.

The numbers that an observer writes down are tabulated in a 10 × 10 matrix as sequence pairs, that is, a separate tabulation is made for each overlapping pair of numbers. An illustration will serve to explain this procedure.

> *Teacher:* "Class! The bell has rung. May I have your attention please!"[6] During the next three seconds talking and noise diminish.[10]
>
> *Teacher:* "Jimmy, we are all waiting for you." [7] Pause.
>
> *Teacher:* "Now today we are going to have a very pleasant surprise, [5] and I think you will find it very exciting and interesting. [1] Have any of you heard anything about what we are going to do?" [4]
>
> *Pupil:* "I think we are going on a trip in the bus that's out in front." [8]
>
> *Teacher:* "Oh! You've found out! How did you learn about our trip?" [4]

By now the observer has written down 6, 10, 7, 5, 1, 4, 8, and 4. As the interaction proceeds, the observer will continue to write down numbers. To tabulate these observations in a 10 × 10 matrix, the first step is to make sure that the entire series begins and ends with the same number. The convention we use is to add a 10 to the beginning and end of the series unless the 10 is already present. Our series now becomes 10, 6, 10, 7, 5, 1, 4, 8, 4, and 10.

These numbers are tabulated in a matrix, one pair at a time. The column is indicated by the second number, the row is indicated by the first number. The first pair is 10-6; the tally is placed in row ten, column six cell. The second pair is 6-10; tally this in the row

TABLE 1

CATEGORIES FOR INTERACTION ANALYSIS

Teacher Talk	Indirect Influence	1.* Accepts Feeling: accepts and clarifies the feeling tone of the students in a nonthreatening manner. Feelings may be positive or negative. Predicting or recalling feelings are included.
		2.* Praises or Encourages: praises or encourages student action or behavior. Jokes that release tension, not at the expense of another individual, nodding head or saying, "um hm?" or "go on" are included.
		3.* Accepts or Uses Ideas of Student: clarifying, building or developing ideas suggested by a student. As teacher brings more of his own ideas into play, shift to category five.
		4.* Asks Questions: asking a question about content or procedure with the intent that a student answer.
	Direct Influence	5.* Lecturing: giving facts or opinions about content or procedures; expressing his own ideas, asking rhetorical questions.
		6.* Giving Directions: directions, commands, or orders with which a student is expected to comply.
		7.* Criticizing or Justifying Authority: statements intended to change student behavior from nonacceptable to acceptable pattern; bawling someone out; stating why the teacher is doing what he is doing; extreme self-reference.
Student Talk		8.* Student Talk—Response: talk by students in response to teacher. Teacher initiates the contact or solicits student statement.
		9.* Student Talk—Initiation: talk by students which they initiate. If "calling on" student is only to indicate who may talk next, observer must decide whether student wanted to talk. If he did, use this category.
		10.* Silence or Confusion: pauses, short periods of silence and periods of confusion in which communication cannot be understood by the observer.

*There is no scale implied by these numbers. Each number is classificatory; it designates a particular kind of communication event. To write these numbers down during observation is to enumerate, not to judge a position on a scale.

58

six, column ten cell. The third pair is 10-7, the fourth pair is 7-5, and so on. Each pair overlaps with the next, and the total number of observations, "N," always will be tabulated by N-1 tallies in the matrix. In this case we started a series of ten numbers, and the series produced nine tallies in the matrix.

Table 2 shows our completed matrix. Notice that in a correctly tabulated matrix the sums of the corresponding rows and columns are equal.

The problem of reliability is extremely complex, and a more complete discussion can be found in two terminal contract reports (6,7) one of which will be published as a research monograph in the 1963 series of the Cooperative Research Program. Education students can learn how to make quick field checks of their reliability and work toward higher reliability under the direction of an instructor.

The Interpretation of Matrices

A matrix should have at least 400 tallies, covering about twenty minutes or more of a homogeneous activity period, before attempting to make an interpretation.

Certain areas within the matrix are particularly useful for describing teacher influence. Some of these areas will now be discussed by making reference to Table 3.

The column totals of a matrix are indicated as Areas "A," "B," "C," and "D." The figures in these areas provide a general picture by answering the following questions: What proportion of the time was someone talking compared with the portion in which confusion or no talking existed? When someone was talking, what proportion of the time was used by the students? By the teacher? Of the time that the teacher talked, what proportion of his talk involved indirect influence? Direct influence?

TABLE 2

Category	1	2	3	4	5	6	7	8	9	10	Total
1				1							1
2											0
3											0
4								1		1	2
5	1										1
6										1	1
7					1						1
8				1							1
9											0
10						1	1				2
Total	1	0	0	2	1	1	1	1	0	2	9

The answers to these questions form a necessary backdrop to the interpretation of the other parts of the matrix. If student participation is about 30 or 40 per cent, we would expect to find out why it was so high by studying the matrix. If the teacher is particularly direct or indirect, we would expect certain relationships to exist with student talk and silence.

The next two areas to consider are areas "E" and "F." Evidence that categories 1, 2, and 3 were used for periods longer than three seconds can be found in the diagonal cells, 1-1, 2-2, and 3-3. The other six cells of Area E indicate various types of transitions between these three categories. Sustained praise or clarification of student ideas is especially significant because such elaboration often involves criteria for praise or reasons for accepting ideas and feelings. The elaboration of praise or student ideas must be present if the student's ideas are to be integrated with the content being discussed by the class.

60

TABLE 3

MATRIX ANALYSIS

Category	Classification		Cate-gory	1	2	3	4	5	6	7	8	9	10	Total
Accepts Feelings	Teacher Talk	Indirect Influence	1											
Praise			2	Area E										
Student Idea			3											
Asks Questions			4				"Content Cross"					Area I		
Lectures		Direct Influence	5											
Gives Directions			6						Area F					
Criticism			7											
Student Response	Student Talk		8	Area G					Area H		Area J			
Student Initiation			9											
Silence			10											
Total														
				Area A				Area B			Area C		Area D	
				Indirect Teacher Talk				Direct Teacher Talk			Student Talk			

61

Area F is a four-cell combination of giving directions (category 6) and giving criticisms or self-justification (category 7). The transition cells 6-7 and 7-6 are particularly sensitive to difficulties that the teacher may have with classroom discipline or resistance on the part of students. When criticism follows directions or direction follows criticism, this means that the students are not complying satisfactorily. Often there is a high loading on the 6-9 cell under these circumstances. Excessively high frequencies in the 6-6 cell *and* 7-7 cells indicate teacher domination and supervision of the students' activities. A high loading of tallies in the 6-6 cell alone often indicates that the teacher is merely giving lengthy directions to the class.

The next two areas to be considered are Areas G and H. Tallies in these two areas occur at the instant the student stops talking and the teacher starts. Area G indicates those instances in which the teacher responds to the termination of student talk with indirect influence. Area H indicates those instances in which the teacher responds to the termination of student talk with direct influence. An interesting comparison can be made by contrasting the proportion G to H versus the proportion A to B. If these two proportions are quite different, it indicates that the teacher tends to act differently at the instant a student stops talking compared with his overall average. Often this is a mark of flexible teacher influence.

There are interesting relationships between Area E and Area G and between Area F and Area H. For example, Area G may indicate that a teacher responds indirectly to students at the instant they terminate their talk, but an observer may wish to inspect Area E to see if this indirect response is sustained in any way. The same question with regard to direct influence can be asked of Areas F and H. Areas G and H together usually fascinate

62

teachers. They are often interested in knowing more about their immediate response to student participation.

Area I indicates an answer to the question, What types of teacher statements trigger student participation? Usually there is a high tally loading in cells 4-8 and 4-9. This is expected because students often answer questions posed by the teacher. A high loading on 4-8 and 8-4 cells alone usually indicates classroom drill directed by the teacher. The contrast of tallies in columns 8 and 9 in this area gives a rough indication of the frequency with which students initiate their own ideas versus respond to those of the teacher.

Area I is often considered in combination with Area J. Area J indicates either lengthy student statements or sustained student-to-student communication. An above-average frequency in Area C, but not in Area J, indicates that short answers, usually in response to teacher stimulation, have occurred. One would normally expect to find frequencies in Area E positively correlated with frequencies in Area J.

We turn next to concepts and principles of teacher influence before speculating about how this technique can be applied to teacher education.

Concepts and Principles of Teacher Influence

It may be too early to determine what are the *fewest* number of concepts which, if organized into logically related principles, can be used by a teacher to plan how he will use his authority. Surely he will need concepts that refer to his authority and its use. He will need concepts to describe learning goals and pupil tasks. He will need concepts to classify the responses of students. He may also need concepts to characterize class formations and patterns of classroom communication. These concepts are at least the minimum.

Concepts That Refer to Teacher Behavior

Indirect influence:—Indirect influence is defined as actions taken by the teacher which encourage and support student participation. Accepting, clarifying, praising, and developing the ideas and feelings expressed by the pupils will support student participation. We can define indirect behavior operationally by noting the per cent of teacher statements falling into categories 1, 2, 3, and 4.

Direct influence:—This concept refers to actions taken by the teacher which restrict student participation. Expressing one's own views through lecture, giving directions, and criticizing with the expectation of compliance tend to restrict pupil participation. We can define direct behavior operationally by noting the per cent of teacher statements falling into categories 5, 6, and 7.

Other concepts which we do not have the space to discuss include: flexibility of teacher influence, dominance or sustained direct influence, and intervention.

Concepts That Refer to Learning Goals

Clear goals:—Goal perceptions are defined from the point of view of the pupil, not the teacher. "Clear goals" is a state of affairs in which the pupil knows what he is doing, the purpose, and can guess at the first few steps to be taken. It can be measured by paper-and-pencil tests, often administered at different points in a problem-solving sequence.

Ambiguous goals:—"Ambiguous goals" describes a state of affairs in which a pupil is not sure of what he is expected to do, is not sure of the first few steps, or is unable to proceed for one reason or another. It can be measured as above.

Other concepts in this area include: attractive and unattractive clear goals, pupil tasks, task requirements, and similar concepts.

Concepts That Refer to Pupil Responses

Dependent acts:—Acts of dependence occur when a pupil not only complies with teacher influence but solicits such direction. A pupil who asks a teacher to approve of his work in order to make sure that it is satisfactory, before going on to the next logical step, is acting dependently. This type of response can be measured by observation techniques and by paper-and-pencil tests on which he indicates what kind of help he would like from the teacher.

Independent acts:—Acts of independence occur when the pupils react primarily to task requirements and are less directly concerned with teacher approval. The measurement of this concept is the same as for dependent acts.

Other concepts include: dependence proneness—a trait, compliance, conformity, counterdependence, and similar concepts.

Some Principles That Can Be Discovered

We discovered in our research (7) that, during the first few days of a two-week unit of study in seventh grade social studies and when introducing new material in eighth grade mathematics, superior teachers (as previously defined, page 252) are initially more indirect, becoming more direct as goals and associated tasks become clarified. We also suspect that these same teachers are more indirect when helping pupils diagnose difficulties, when trying to motivate pupils by arousing their interest, and in other situations in which the expression of pupil perceptions is helpful. On the other hand, the average or below average teacher did exactly the opposite.

Now the problem in teacher education is

not only to create a situation in which education students could verify these relationships but could practice controlling their own behavior so as to become indirect or more direct at will. One place to begin is to have two, six-man groups work on a task under the direction of a leader. One task is something like an assembly line; it has a clear end product and sharp role differentiation. The other task is much more difficult to describe and does not have clear role differentiation. Now let the class superimpose different patterns of leader influence. Let them interview the role players, collect interaction analysis data by some simplified system of categories, and discuss the results. When undergraduate students first try to classify verbal statements, it sometimes helps to use only two or three categories. In one instance, the issue was the effect of using broad questions versus narrow questions. A broad question was one to which it was hard to predict the type of answer. A narrow question was one to which it was easy to guess at the type of answer. Which type of question was more likely to increase pupil participation? The students role-played this and kept a record of broad questions, narrow questions, and the length of the response. The fact that they verified their prediction correctly for this rather superficial problem was much less important compared with the experience that they gained. They learned how to verify a prediction with empirical evidence, and some had a chance to practice control of their own behavior for professional purposes.

There is no space here to list a complete set of principles that can be investigated by systematic or intuitive data-collecting procedures. The following questions might stimulate useful learning activities. Does dependence always decrease as goals become clear? Is the final level of dependence determined by the pattern of teacher influence when goals are first formulated? Are measures of content achievement related to the pupils' attitudes toward the teacher and the schoolwork? What effects can you expect from excessive and pedantic clarification of pupil ideas and feelings? And many others.

Applications of Interaction Analysis to Teacher Education

Suppose that before education students were given their practice teaching assignment, they had been exposed to a variety of data-collecting techniques for assessing pupil perceptions, measuring achievement, and quantifying spontaneous teacher influence. Suppose, further, that these skills had been taught in a context of personal inquiry as described earlier. What effect would this have on their approach to practice teaching?

One of their suggestions might be that two students should be assigned as a team to the first assignment. While one took over the class the other could be collecting information; the next day or so, the roles could be reversed. Together they would work out a lesson plan, agree on the data to be collected, go over the results with the help of the supervising teacher who might also have the same data-collecting skills. This situation could approach the inquiry model described earlier. The practice teacher might discover that his failure to clarify the pupils' ideas restricted the development of curiosity or that his directions were too short when he was asked for further help; both of these inferences can be made from an interaction matrix with reasonable reliability and objectivity.

Later on a student may wish to take a practice teaching assignment by himself and turn to the supervising teacher for aid in feedback. In either case, the requirement is that the learner be able to compare his intentions with feedback information about his actions and

67

analyze this information by using concepts which he found useful in his earlier courses in education.

There are some precautions that can already be stated with regard to the use of interaction analysis in such a situation.

First, no interaction analysis data should be collected unless the person observed is familiar with the entire process and knows its limitations.

Second, the questions to be answered by inspecting the matrix should be developed before the observation takes place.

Third, value judgments about good and bad teaching behavior are to be avoided. Emphasis is given to the problem being investigated so that cause-and-effect relationships can be discovered.

Fourth, a certain amount of defensive behavior is likely to be present at the initial consultation; it is something like listening to a tape recording for the first time.

Fifth, a consultation based on two observations or at least two matrices helps to eliminate value judgments or at least control them. Comparisons between the matrices are more likely to lead to principles.

Just how experiences of the type we have been discussing will fit into the present curricula is difficult to know. If activities of the sort described in this paper are valuable, are they to be superimposed on the present list of courses or is more radical surgery necessary?

Perhaps this is the point to risk a prediction, which is that teacher education will become increasingly concerned with the process of teaching itself during the next few decades. Instead of emphasizing knowledge which *we think* teachers will need in order to teach effectively, as we have in the past, we will turn more and more to an analysis of teaching acts as they occur in spontaneous classroom interaction. We are now at the point in our technology of data collecting at which procedures for analyzing and conceptualizing teaching behavior can be developed. Systems for doing this will become available regardless of whether they are similar or dissimilar to the procedures described in this paper. When this fine day arrives, the role of the education instructor will change, and the dichotomy between field and theory will disappear. The instructor's role will shift from talking about effective teaching to the rigorous challenge of demonstrating effective teaching. The process of inquiry will create problem-solving activities that will produce more independent, self-directing teachers whose first day on the job will be their worst, not their best.

These changes will be successful to the extent that the graduates of teacher education can learn to control their own behavior for the professional purpose of managing effective classroom learning. It will be the responsibility of the education instructor to help prospective teachers discover what their teaching intentions should be and then create training situations in which behavior gradually matches intentions with practice. Teaching will remain an art, but it will be studied scientifically.

REFERENCES

1. Anderson, Harold H. "The Measurement of Domination and of Socially Integrative Behavior in Teachers' Contacts with Children." *Child Development* 10: 73-89; June 1939.
2. ———, and Brewer, Helen M. *Studies of Teachers' Classroom Personalities, I: Dominative and Socially Integrative Behavior of Kindergarten Teachers.* Applied Psychology Monographs of the American Psychological Association. No. 6. Stanford, California: Stanford University Press, July 1945.
3. ———, and Brewer, Joseph E. *Studies of Teachers' Classroom Personalities, II: Effects of Teachers' Dominative and Integrative Contacts on Children's Classroom. Behavior.* Applied Psychology Monographs of the American Psychological Association. No. 8. Stanford, California: Stanford University Press, June 1946.
4. ———; Brewer, J. E.; and Reed, M. F. *Studies of Teachers' Classroom Personalities, III: Follow-up Studies of the Effects of Dominative and Integrative Contacts on Children's Behavior.* Applied Psychology

Monographs of the American Psychological Association. No. 11. Stanford, California: Stanford University Press, December 1946.

5. Cantor, Nathaniel. *The Teaching-Learning Process.* New York: Dryden Press, 1953. pp. 59-72.

6. Flanders, N. A. A terminal contract report on using interaction analysis for the inservice training of teachers. To be submitted to the U.S. Office of Education, N.D.E.A., Title VII. Available from the author, University of Michigan, after April 1963.

7. ————. *Teacher Influence, Pupil Attitudes, and Achievement.* Dittoed manuscript to be published in 1963 as a Research Monograph, Cooperative Research Program, U.S. Office of Education. Available from author, University of Michigan, 1962. 176 pp.

8. ————, and Havumaki, S. "Group Compliance to Dominative Teacher Influence." *Human Relations* 13:67-82.

9. Romney, G. P.; Hughes, M. M.; and others. *Progress Report of the Merit Study of the Provo City Schools.* Provo, Utah, August 1958. XIX + 226 pp. See also *Patterns of Effective Teaching: Second Progress Report of the Merit Study of the Provo City Schools.* Provo, Utah, June 1961. XII + 93 pp.

10. Thelen, H. A. *Education and the Human Quest.* New York: Harper Brothers, 1960. pp. 74-112.

THE USE OF VIDEOTAPE RECORDINGS IN THE ANALYSIS OF STUDENT TEACHING PERFORMANCE

Charles R. DuVall and Wayne J. Krepel

The use of videotape equipment in schools, particularly in the analysis and evaluation of teaching performance, is a procedure which is of comparatively recent origin. It does, however, have several possibilities which should be explored in depth, particularly in relationship to broadening and increasing the effectiveness of the student teaching supervisor, and concomitantly the training of the student teacher. This article is a report of one method, directly involving the use of videotaping of teaching, which has been utilized by the authors. The report is far from complete, and the method is far from perfected. This, then, is an interim report; but it has been effective for both student teachers and supervisors.

The basic procedure utilized is a combination of on-site visitation (traditional) on a somewhat regular basis and the supplementary use of videotaping of selected lessons. In these videotaping sessions the supervisor (and in about half the cases, the cooperating teacher) is not present, but rather a trained technician (a work-study student) is present in the classroom for filming the lesson.

One basic assumption in this method is that evaluation does not act as a barrier to communication between teachers and supervisors; rather, the total process of evaluation is an effective aid in initiating and maintaining open lines of communication. The students, knowing that they will have the opportunity to see and evaluate their own teaching performance, will actively seek out and maintain effective methods of communication. Lindemann found that teachers who perceived that they were being evaluated communicated more frequently with their supervisors than did teachers who believed they were not being evaluated. (4, p. 207)

The procedure by the authors here departs from certain traditional supervisory practices in that the student teacher does have the

THE TEACHER EDUCATOR, Autumn 1971, pp. 12-16.

opportunity to see himself teach, yet he is not required to share this taped experience with his college supervisor. That is, the supervisor views the tape with the student only at the student's request. It is believed that this option gives the student a sense of security which he might not otherwise have were he required to share his tape with the supervisor. To date, within the limited experience available to the authors, no student has failed to request the supervisor to share his tape.

Following the videotaping of the lesson, usually of twenty minutes to one-half hour in duration, the student is afforded the opportunity for immediate feedback. Both Peter and Schreiner (6, p. 23) and Elliott and Markham (2, pp. 46-48) found that immediate feedback played an important part in the evaluation process. In addition to the positive effects for the student teacher there is also a second advantage which the authors believe cannot be overlooked. The school systems and the teachers dealt with in our student teaching program are not very familiar with videotaping. Hence, the student may overreact to the presence of the equipment and the operator's presence in the classroom. We have attempted to overcome, or at least mitigate, this effect in the following ways: (1) the use of a directional microphone mounted on the camera and the placement of a second microphone on a pedestal in the front of the room, as opposed to the use of a lavaliere mike, and (2) bringing playback equipment into the classroom so the students may view themselves immediately. We do this in order that the student teacher may have the advantage of immediate playback, but it also permits the students to see themselves. Contrary to the belief of some, we think that this procedure tends to cut down on students misbehaving before the camera. They know that they will see themselves immediately; hence, they behave in a more normal manner.

There are two disadvantages which have occurred when utilizing the above procedures. The first is that the technician must not only transport the recording equipment, he must also bring along playback equipment. This necessitates a large screen set being transported into the school. The second disadvantage is that, particularly in the high school, the timing of the lesson must not run much over one-half of the period. This is necessary in order to afford the students, who have been promised the playback, the opportunity to view themselves on television.

Following the immediate playback in the classroom, the student teacher is then afforded the opportunity to view his teaching performance at his leisure. Viewing carrels are provided at the university where the student can engage in the self-analysis of his teaching performance. This is accomplished without the presence of either the cooperating teacher or the college supervisor. At this time the opportunity is given the student teacher to erase his tape if he wishes. Students are encouraged to view their tapes within forty-eight hours after they are made. In no case is a period of longer than five days allowed for this particular activity.

Following this self-analytic viewing it is possible for the university supervisor to view the tape if the student gives his permission. This may be done either with the student present or at the supervisor's convenience. This viewing offers the student teacher and the university supervisor an opportunity to hold a critique of the experience. The authors are convinced that students tend to be far more harsh in the evaluation of their own teaching performance than are either the cooperating teacher or the university supervisor.

This technique of supervision also has one advantage to the supervisor and his colleagues at the university, particularly those teaching methods courses. It is possible to utilize videotapes of student teaching performances and pupil classroom behavior to illustrate to undergraduate classes particular behavioral and response patterns. This technique may be viewed as a modified micro-teaching or microviewing experience. Here the only caution which must be exercised is that of obtaining the permission of the student teacher to use his performance for illustrative purposes within the university classroom. The authors believe that if only positive segments of videotaped teaching performances are shown, that is, those in which student teachers are used as illustrative models of positive teaching behavior, the undergraduate student may lose some fears of videotaping. This particular application of videotaping is now at the trial stage at Indiana University at South Bend.

In summary, the procedure can be stated briefly as follows:

1. Student teacher, university supervisor, and cooperating teacher must all agree that videotaping will be a worthwhile educational experience. Either the student or the cooperating teacher may elect not to utilize this technique.

2. The student is given the opportunity to prepare his "video lesson" in advance. This is necessary because of scheduling demands and requirements. Normally, the equipment is scheduled to be set up either before school begins or at recess periods in the elementary schools, or during the conference or open hour in the high school.

3. A trained technician, usually a work-study student at the university, videotapes the class session. The university supervisor and cooperating teacher are usually not in the classroom during the actual videotaping of the lesson.

4. Videotaping time usually does not exceed thirty minutes. This limit is necessary because of the length of tape and the length of the class periods. It is the belief of the authors that this is sufficient time to acquire material for purposes of self-analysis.

5. Immediate playback is afforded the student teacher and the pupils. The cooperating teacher is usually invited to this session.

6. The student teacher then views his videotape at his leisure in a carrel at the university.

7. The student teacher may erase his videotape after this viewing if he so desires.

8. The student teacher may ask his university supervisor to view the videotape. The videotape then becomes the means for an analysis of the student teacher's skill.

9. The videotapes may also be used, with the student's permission, in selected classes.

Some of the disadvantages are:

1. Due to the necessity for advance scheduling of the equipment in the schools the student teacher and the pupils may not react in an entirely normal and spontaneous manner. This may be especially true during the first videotaping session.

2. To utilize the immediate playback option it is necessary to transport playback equipment to the site of the videotaping.

3. Class time limits, particularly at the high school level, may restrict videotaping and lesson planning options available to the student teacher.

4. The student teacher may view his videotaped lesson as more of a performance than a teaching activity.

Finally, the apparent advantages of a program such as the one suggested by the authors are:

1. Supervision and evaluation aid communication between the student teacher and his supervisor.

2. Videotaping can and should serve as a basis for discussion and analysis among the student teacher and his pupils, the cooperating teacher, and the university supervisor.

3. The "erase tape" option removes much of the pressure usually associated with videotaping.

74

4. The videotape may provide a variety of video materials for other instructional purposes within the university.

References

1. Adair, Charles H., and R. Kyle Allen, "Effects of Feedbacks on Teacher Behavior, An Exploration into the Use of Videotaping in Teacher Education Programs," *Research in Education*, V, May 1971, 95.
2. Elliot, Richard B., and David H. Markham, "Portable Video Recorders in Higher Education," *Audiovisual Instruction*, XV, December 1970, 46-48.
3. Johnson, James A., and Clair R. Tettemer, "The Use of Portable Videotaping Equipment in Teacher Education," *Audiovisual Instruction*, XV, April 1970, 108-10.
4. Lindemann, Bertram C., "Teacher Evaluation: Barrier to Communication?" *Educational Leadership*, XXVIII, November 1970, 207-8.
5. Mueller, Gene, "The Videotape for Self-Evaluation," *Today's Education*, LIX, January 1970, 39.
6. Peters, David R., and Philip J. Schreiner, "The Effects of Television and Expert Feedback on Self-Perception," *Research in Education*, VI, January 1971, 23.
7. Ward, Phillip M., "The Use of Portable Videotape Recorder in Helping Teachers Self-Evaluate Their Teaching Behavior," *Research in Education*, VIII, August 1970, 104.

CLASSROOM CONTROL
Should be a vital part
of teacher education

By DONALD A. WESLEY

"Teaching might be fun if it wasn't for the kids," was a wistful remark once made by a downhearted novice. It is well-known that the ability to maintain order is one of the greatest challenges faced by new teachers. Nothing has more to do with their future success and happiness. Since the importance of the subject has long been recognized, one may assume that considerable attention is paid to it in the training of teachers. This assumption should raise two significant questions. First, from what sources does the prospective teacher learn about discipline, and secondly, how effective is the instruction that takes place?

Briefly, here are six possible sources of information. First, classroom control is treated in educational methods classes at the college or university. Here, the student may benefit from the experience of the instructor, and also read about the subject. The other source of information at this level is the college supervisor of student teaching. He, too, may have had much practical experience in public school classrooms. In the cooperating school the supervising teacher is the key source of information. Probably no other individual is in a better position to offer advice. While the student is in the school

there is often the opportunity to observe classes, and also to discuss disciplinary matters with other teachers, the principal, or the department chairman. Students also find time to share experiences and suggestions with each other in the same way as veteran teachers are known to do. Finally, it must be noted that a number of educators believe that discipline is not something that can be taught at all, but is to be learned only through experience. This, too, must then be considered as a source.

There are specific shortcomings which hinder effective instruction about classroom discipline by all of the above sources. For instance, the information that is acquired in the educational methods class is illustrative. As this is frequently a course taken prior to the senior year, the student may forget much of what is learned before he actually begins teaching. Furthermore, the topic may not be taken seriously or have relevance for him due to this early exposure. There is also some question as to whether classroom control can be treated in the same manner as other topics. Students make lesson plans, construct examinations, and perform a host of other activities in this class, but there is little or no opportunity for

THE CLEARING HOUSE, 1971, Vol. 45, pp. 346-349.

them to demonstrate classroom management. At best there is discussion and some questions are answered.

How much time an instructor devotes to the subject is determined by how important it is to him. Insufficient coverage will occur if it is believed that the only place to learn discipline is out in the schools, or if the professor is convinced that good teaching will eliminate it from the classroom. Others, more naive, pretend classroom problems are uncommon, and that either the child or the teacher is disturbed.[1]

Certain resources are at the disposal of the methods professor. Most commonplace are the textbooks which ordinarily include a chapter on classroom discipline. In addition, valuable articles are found in the educational periodicals. Though much can be gained from this kind of reading, some of the material is too theoretical and unpractical. Many instructors draw upon their own public school teaching experience in dealing with discipline, and there is much to commend in this approach. One minor criticism is that experience can grow less vivid with each passing year. Unfortunately, some methods professors have taught only briefly in the public schools, if at all. It is obvious that their coverage may very well be superficial.

Discipline is also a topic of considerable interest to the college supervisor of student teaching. The amount of assistance that he is able to give the student teacher again depends on his own experience, and how long he has been supervising. He is in direct contact with the public school classroom, and does see the teacher and pupil in a live teaching situation. Often the college supervisor directs a seminar for student teachers and is able to spend much time on the subject.

Many believe that the supervising teacher is the individual who has the most responsibility in teaching the art of discipline to novices. Of course, much depends on whether or not this person is a capable disciplinarian. It is most unfortunate for the student teacher if it proves otherwise. Actually, first-year teachers are rarely employed as supervisors because many are often occupied themselves in learning classroom control. Occasionally supervising teachers are utilized who have unorthodox ideas, or who employ questionable practices. Obviously these people can cause problems for student teachers.

Observing teachers in action by visiting their classrooms may be beneficial. It must be recognized, however, that it is not often that such classes will have discipline problems with a visitor present. Pupils will act naturally if they are accustomed to having observers. Though it is enlightening to note how other teachers handle various situations, the students must recognize that there might be several ways to deal with a specific problem. They must be aware that what works for someone else may prove ineffective for them. Differing personalities and length of experience should be taken into consideration. I once knew of a supervising teacher who merely wrote "QUIET" on the chalkboard to get the desired result. When the student teacher attempted this, the noise actually increased.

Certainly student teachers can learn from sharing ideas with one another. However, in some instances this can be likened to "the blind leading the blind," as one can criticize such advice from the standpoint of lack of experience.[2]

What about the viewpoint that the only way to learn discipline is through experience? Most educators will support the contention that, as in any other occupation, there is nothing superior to on-the-job training. Learning to be an effective disciplinarian is no exception. Many teachers scoff at what they learned about classroom control from any other source except from experience.

Valuable as the experience theory is, it can be carried too far. It can lead to leaving the student teacher or first year teacher to his fate. A similar comparison is teaching a person how to swim by tying a rope around his middle and casting him into a river. Underlying this position is the thought that only the fit will and should survive. It is unfortunate that such thinking still persists. It has prevented any number of would-be teachers from entering the profession who might have succeeded if they had been given some self-confidence coupled with understanding.

Thus the prospective teacher does come in contact with disciplinary instruction through a number of sources. Much of what he reads, sees, and hears will certainly become more meaningful when he actually faces youngsters in a classroom. However, it should be surprising to know that some student teachers and first-year teachers do not take seriously what they heard about discipline during their college years. Consider the time-tested adage of advising the neophyte to lean toward strictness at first and to ease up later when conditions warrant.[3] A young novice once confided that he had listened to this advice for three years, and never did take it seriously. However, he had since become involved in a situation where his disregard for this warning had caused him to lose the respect of his class. He had never been able to reestablish control to any degree. This young man had to wait another year to learn the wisdom of the recommended approach.

Like most veteran teachers, some student teachers will prove to be natural disciplinarians. They may require less instruction, but certainly there is much for them to learn. However, those who are not "naturals" can learn to become effective disciplinarians. This is not the result of merely following principles or rules; no money-back guarantee comes with any of them. The so-called "tricks of the trade" are not infallible. Nevertheless, being exposed to them can be most helpful.

What suggestions can be made to those involved with teaching discipline?

(1) While it is recognized that good teaching does reduce behavioral problems, it does not eliminate all of them. Therefore, in educational methods classes, discipline should be looked upon as a topic of paramount importance. It should have as much time allotment as does lesson planning or any other subject.

(2) Instructors who teach these courses ought to have a considerable amount of recent classroom experience. Ideally, "clinical professors" would be the most suitable.[4] Such individuals would be expected to "practice what they preach." In the absence of clinical professors it would be worthwhile to require methods instructors to supervise some student teachers as part of their load. This should help make their discussion of discipline more realistic and meaningful. In addition, there would be the opportunity to observe the implementation of practices recommended or advised in the college classroom. A similar suggestion is that methods professors teach a public school class for a semester every few years. There is little doubt that this experience would have a significant effect on their college instruction!

(3) Methods professors and college supervisors conducting seminars should employ a variety of materials and teaching techniques when dealing with the topic of discipline. Using micro-teaching and video-taping, developing an up-to-date bibliography and film list, employing case studies and role-playing, are just a few approaches. One novel technique requires methods students to present half-hour lessons to their peers.[5] In addition to being an excellent all-around learning experience, it also provides the opportunity to handle disciplinary matters. Members of the class may occasionally "commit" infractions such as whispering, rising to sharpen a pencil during a discussion, or asking inane questions. Though this process is somewhat unrealistic, students have often admitted that they had not realized that classroom control was that closely related to teaching.

(4) Supervising teachers should be selected with an eye to their effectiveness as disciplinarians. If this is ignored or overlooked, it can have serious consequences for the novice.

(5) Students observing teachers in the classroom should be specifically directed to note conditions that may cause disturbances, how problems are handled, alternative methods that could have been employed, and other items. These should be followed up by discussion in the methods class or seminar.

(6) In conclusion, in getting the most from his own experience during student teaching, the novice must profit from whatever disciplinary mistakes that are made. Some of these may be pointed out while others he hopefully will discover alone. This awareness, coupled with past instruction, and a genuine appreciation of youngsters, will enable the prospective teacher to begin a career with confidence and assurance.

FOOTNOTES

1. James Raths et al., Studying Teaching (Englewood Cliffs, New Jersey: Prentice-Hall Book Company, 1967), p. 407.

2. See Robert J. Griffin, "Student Teachers Can Learn From Each Other," Peabody Journal of Education, 32:283–89, March, 1955, for a contrary view.

3. This admonition is not always supported. See Donald R. Waldrip, "Get Tough in the Beginning and then Relax—Nonsense!" Phi Delta Kappan 47: 308–309, February, 1966.

4. Clinical professors are discussed in James B. Conant, The Education of American Teachers (New York City, N.Y.: McGraw-Hill Book Company, 1963).

5. For a more detailed discussion, see Donald A. Wesley, "Try-Out Teaching in Secondary Methods Courses," Peabody Journal of Education, 39:46–49, July, 1961.

CLASSROOM MANAGEMENT

TEACHERS' EXPECTANCIES: DETERMINANTS OF PUPILS' IQ GAINS[1]

ROBERT ROSENTHAL   AND   LENORE JACOBSON

Summary.—Within each of 18 classrooms, an average of 20% of the children were reported to classroom teachers as showing unusual potential for intellectual gains. Eight months later these "unusual" children (who had actually been selected at random) showed significantly greater gains in IQ than did the remaining children in the control group. These effects of teachers' expectancies operated primarily among the younger children.

Experiments have shown that in behavioral research employing human or animal Ss, E's expectancy can be a significant determinant of S's response (Rosenthal, 1964, in press). In studies employing animals, for example, Es led to believe that their rat Ss had been bred for superior learning ability obtained performance superior to that obtained by Es led to believe their rats had been bred for inferior learning ability (Rosenthal & Fode, 1963; Rosenthal & Lawson, 1964). The present study was designed to extend the generality of this finding from Es to teachers and from animal Ss to school children.

Flanagan (1960) has developed a nonverbal intelligence test (*Tests of General Ability* or *TOGA*) which is not explicitly dependent on such school-learned skills as reading, writing, and arithmetic. The test is composed of two types of items, "verbal" and "reasoning." The "verbal" items measure the child's level of information, vocabulary, and concepts. The "reasoning" items measure the child's concept formation ability by employing abstract line drawings. Flanagan's purpose in developing the TOGA was "to provide a relatively fair measure of intelligence for all individuals, even those who have had atypical opportunities to learn" (1960, p. 6).

Flanagan's test was administered to all children in an elementary school, disguised as a test designed to predict academic "blooming" or intellectual gain. Within each of the six grades in the school were three classrooms, one each of children performing at above average, average, and below average levels of scholastic achievement. In each of the 18 classes an average of 20% of the children were assigned to the experimental condition. The names of these children were

[1]This research was supported by Research Grants GS-177 and GS-714 from Division of Social Sciences of the National Science Foundation. We thank Dr. Paul Nielsen, Superintendent, South San Francisco Unified School District, for making this study possible; Dr. David Marlowe for his valuable advice; and Mae Evans, Nancy Johnson, John Laszlo, Susan Novick, and George Smiltens for their assistance. A more extended treatment of this material will be published by Holt, Rinehart and Winston as a chapter in a book tentatively entitled *Social Class, Race, and Psychological Development.*

PSYCHOLOGICAL REPORTS, 1966, vol. 19, pp. 115-118.

given to each teacher who was told that their scores on the "test for intellectual blooming" indicated that they would show unusual intellectual gains during the academic year. Actually, the children had been assigned to the experimental condition by means of a table of random numbers. The experimental treatment for these children, then, consisted of nothing more than being identified to their teachers as children who would show unusual intellectual gains.

Eight months after the experimental conditions were instituted all children were retested with the same IQ test and a change score was computed for each child. Table 1 shows the mean gain in IQ points among experimental and con-

TABLE 1
MEAN GAINS IN IQ

Grade	Controls		Experimentals		Diff.	t	p†
	M	σ	M	σ			
1	12.0	16.6	27.4	12.5	15.4	2.97	.002
2	7.0	10.0	16.5	18.6	9.5	2.28	.02
3	5.0	11.9	5.0	9.3	0.0		
4	2.2	13.4	5.6	11.0	3.4		
5	17.5	13.1	17.4	17.8	−0.1		
6	10.7	10.0	10.0	6.5	−0.7		
Weighted M	8.4*	13.5	12.2**	15.0	3.8	2.15	.02

*Mean number of children per grade = 42.5.
**Mean number of children per grade = 10.8.
†p one-tailed.

trol Ss in each of the six grades.[2] For the school as a whole those children from whom the teachers had been led to expect greater intellectual gain showed a significantly greater gain in IQ score than did the control children ($p = .02$, one-tail). Inspection of Table 1 shows that the effects of teachers' expectancies were not uniform across the six grade levels. The lower the grade level, the greater was the effect ($rho = −.94$, $p = .02$, two-tail). It was in the first and second grades that the effects were most dramatic. The largest gain among the three first grade classrooms occurred for experimental Ss who gained 24.8 IQ points *in excess* of the gain ($+16.2$) shown by the controls. The largest gain among the three second grade classrooms was obtained by experimental Ss who gained 18.2 IQ points in excess of the gain ($+4.3$) shown by the controls.

An additionally useful way of showing the effects of teachers' expectancies on their pupils' gains in IQ is to show the percentage of experimental and control Ss achieving various magnitudes of gains. Table 2 shows such percentages

[2]There were no differences in the effects of teachers' expectancies as a function of Ss' initial level of educational achievement; therefore, the three classrooms at each grade level were combined for Table 1. In one of the three classrooms at the fifth grade level, a portion of the IQ test was inadvertently not re-administered so that data of Table 1 are based on 17 instead of 18 classrooms.

TABLE 2

PERCENTAGES OF EXPERIMENTAL AND CONTROL Ss GAINING 10, 20, OR 30
IQ POINTS (FIRST AND SECOND GRADE CHILDREN)

IQ Gain	Control Ss*	Experimental Ss**	χ^2	p†
10 points	49	79	4.75	.02
20 points	19	47	5.59	.01
30 points	5	21	3.47	.04

*Total number of children = 95.
**Total number of children = 19.
†p one-tailed.

for the first and second grades only. Half again as many experimental as control Ss gained at least 10 IQ points; more than twice as many gained at least 20 IQ points; and more than four times as many gained at least 30 points.

An important question was whether the gains of the experimental Ss were made at the expense of the control Ss. Tables 1 and 2 show that control Ss made substantial gains in IQ though they were smaller than the gains made by experimental Ss. Better evidence for the proposition that gains by experimental Ss were not made at the expense of control Ss comes from the positive correlation between gains made by experimental and control Ss. Over the 17 classrooms in which the comparison was possible, those in which experimental Ss made greater gains tended also to be the ones where control Ss made greater gains ($rho =$ .57, $p = .02$, two-tail).

Retesting of the children's IQ had been done in classroom groups by the children's own teacher.[3] The question arose, therefore, whether the greater gain in IQ of the experimental children might have been due to the teacher's differential behavior toward them during the retesting. To help answer this question three of the classes were retested by a school administrator not attached to the particular school. She did not know which children were in the experimental condition. Results based on her retesting of the children were not significantly different from the results based on the children's own teachers' retesting. In fact, there was a tendency for the results of her retesting to yield even larger effects of teachers' expectancies. It appears unlikely, then, that the greater IQ gains made by children from whom greater gains were expected could be attributed to the effect of the behavior of the teacher while she served as an examiner.

There are a number of possible explanations of the finding that teachers' expectancy effects operated primarily at the lower grade levels, including: (a) Younger children have less well-established reputations so that the creation of expectations about their performance would be more credible. (b) Younger children may be more susceptible to the unintended social influence exerted by the expectation of their teacher. (c) Younger children may be more recent

[3]Scoring of the tests was done by the investigators, not by the teachers.

arrivals in the school's neighborhood and may differ from the older children in characteristics other than age. (d) Teachers of lower grades may differ from teachers of higher grades on a variety of dimensions which are correlated with the effectiveness of the unintentional communication of expectancies.

The most important question which remains is that which asks how a teacher's expectation becomes translated into behavior in such a way as to elicit the expected pupil behavior. Prior research on the unintentional communication of expectancies in experimentally more carefully controlled interactions suggests that this question will not be easily answered (Rosenthal, in press).

But, regardless of the mechanism involved, there are important substantive and methodological implications of these findings which will be discussed in detail elsewhere. For now, one example, in question form, will do: How much of the improvement in intellectual performance attributed to the contemporary educational programs is due to the content and methods of the programs and how much is due to the favorable expectancies of the teachers and administrators involved? Experimental designs to answer such questions are available (Rosenthal, in press) and in view of the psychological, social and economic importance of these programs the use of such designs seems strongly indicated.

REFERENCES

FLANAGAN, J. C. *Tests of general ability: technical report.* Chicago, Ill.: Science Research Associates, 1960.

ROSENTHAL, R. The effect of the experimenter on the results of psychological research. In B. A. Maher (Ed.), *Progress in experimental personality research.* Vol. I. New York: Academic Press, 1964. Pp. 79-114.

ROSENTHAL, R. *Experimenter effects in behavioral research.* New York: Appleton-Century-Crofts, in press.

ROSENTHAL, R., & FODE, K. L. The effect of experimenter bias on the performance of the albino rat. *Behavioral Science,* 1963, 8, 183-189.

ROSENTHAL, R., & LAWSON, R. A longitudinal study of the effects of experimenter bias on the operant learning of laboratory rats. *Journal of Psychiatric Research,* 1964, 2, 61-72.

THE SELF-FULFILLING PROPHECY

THOMAS L. GOOD *and* JERE E. BROPHY

☐ **Publicity about "Pygmalion in the Classroom"** [a 1968 Holt publication by Robert Rosenthal and Lenore Jacobson that describes the now-famous study in which the authors found that teacher expectations affect pupil achievement] has aroused much interest and created a good deal of confusion. Some popularized accounts of the book have been misleading, seeming to imply that the mere existence of an expectation will automatically and mysteriously guarantee its fulfillment. Teachers rightly recognize this idea as utter nonsense and reject it. Unfortunately, however, they sometimes then reject completely the concept of the self-fulfilling prophecy.

During the second semester of the 1969-70 school year, we carried out research that leads us to say that sometimes teachers' expectations do, indeed, function as self-fulfilling prophecies. But we wish to make clear that when we say this, we do *not* mean that any expectation is, ipso facto, going to come true. We *do* mean that teachers' expectations can affect their behavior and that their behavior will in turn affect the children by communicating these expectations to them.

In our study, we observed four first grade classrooms after the teachers had had time to get to know their children well. We made no attempt to influence the expectations of the teachers; instead we simply asked them to rank the children in their class in order

TODAY'S EDUCATION—NEA JOURNAL, April 1971, pp. 52-53.

of achievement. In each of the four rooms, we selected from these lists for special observation three boys and three girls who ranked high and three boys and three girls who ranked low. Our interest was in discovering whether or not the teachers treated the highs and the lows differently in ways that were predictable from the self-fulfilling prophecy hypothesis. The findings were quite clear: Differential treatment of the two groups consistent with the hypothesis occurred in all four classrooms.

Particularly instructive are certain findings concern- ing the teachers' behavior when the children were reading aloud in the reading group or attempting to answer teacher questions. In both situations, the teachers tended to treat the two groups of children differently when they were "stuck" or when they had given a wrong answer. When dealing with high expectation pupils in such instances, the teachers tended **to repeat the question, rephrase the question, give a clue, or ask another question**—reactions that involve working with the child and giving him a second chance to respond to the same question or to a related one. With the low expectation pupils, the teachers tended to give the answer or call on someone else, thereby closing off the interaction.

There were also striking differences in the teachers' reactions to the children's responses. Even though the highs gave many more right answers and fewer wrong ones than the lows, they were twice as likely to receive praise for a correct response and only one-third as likely to receive criticism for an incorrect response. And there was a clear difference in the frequency with which the teachers failed to give any kind of reaction to the child. This absence of teacher reaction occurred in only 3 percent of the interactions with the highs, whereas it occurred in 18 percent of those with the lows.

Teacher behavior flowing from low expectations interferes with progress in two ways.

First, it limits the amount of material that a child can learn—partly because his teachers do not try to **teach him as much and partly because they give up much more easily and quickly in teaching him the things they do try to teach.**

Second, such behavior stifles a pupil's motivation and gives him a feeling of alienation. (Not surprisingly, the highs in our study sought out the teacher to discuss their work about five times as often as the lows.) If anything, we might expect the teacher to be on the lookout for chances to encourage the lows by praising the success that they do attain and would, at the same time, be slow to criticize them in view of their greater learning difficulty.

The sad state of affairs we observed in these four classrooms apparently is the end result of a gradual process that, in all probability, begins when initial difficulties in teaching the lows erode the teacher's confidence in his ability to teach them. This leads him eventually to adopt the attitude that these children are unable to learn like the others. As the attitude becomes more firmly established, failure expectations likewise become firmly established.

Gradually, things get to the point where the teacher "knows" in advance that certain children will not learn the lesson. He no longer expects to teach the lows in the sense of working with them until they master the material. Instead, unconsciously abandoning serious teaching efforts, he halfheartedly goes through the motions of teaching just long enough to reassure himself that the children indeed cannot learn.

Under such circumstances, the teacher is naturally more tuned to evidence of failure than of success in the lows. He may not notice when these children *are* doing good work or when they *are* paying attention. Consequently, he misses opportunities to encourage them and to stimulate new learning. He focuses attention on their failures and finally functions as a carping critic rather than as an encouraging instructor.

None of this process is deliberate. The teachers we observed were surprised and distressed when we told them what we had found. They were open to suggestion and correction, realizing that even the best teachers need and benefit from feedback.

Unfortunately, however, because expectations guide both perceptions and behavior, their self-perpetuating capacity is very strong. Being human, all teachers are much more likely to see what they expect to find than what they don't expect to find. And all too frequently they fail to test their assumptions in the classroom, which often leads them to accept needlessly low performance from students. Certainly if they never check their assumptions, they are not going to change.

The central issue here is the importance of teacher attitude. IQ scores and other sources of information are neither bad nor good, per se. The use that the teacher makes of the information is what is crucial. Of vital importance is that he see information about a child as merely hypothesis—the best guess at the moment.

In conclusion, let us identify those desirable teacher attitudes and expectations that are inextricably linked with effective teaching:

1. The teacher believes that skill acquisition is the major (though not the only) goal of the program and that deliberate instruction is a major responsibility of the teacher.

2. The teacher genuinely and seriously expects all children to meet at least the minimal program objectives and is willing to spend extra time with the children who have difficulty.

3. The teacher understands that the crucial aspects of the teaching role are instruction, diagnosis, and remediation rather than the giving of directions and evaluations.

4. The teacher expects to talk to and with the children, not merely at them.

5. The teacher realizes that when his behavior is appropriate, his pupils will find skill acquisition inherently enjoyable and rewarding.

Teaching is a very complex activity, but teachers who enjoy children, who have mastered basic teaching techniques, and who are open to corrective feedback are well on their way toward becoming outstanding teachers.

IQ:
GOD-GIVEN
OR MAN-MADE?

By GILBERT VOYAT

WHO would have believed that in the declining decades of the twentieth century the antique psychological argument between environment and heredity would garner headlines and rub academic tempers raw? The older, progressive educators scolded each other about the primacy of nurture over nature. The practicing pragmatists insisted that, "You are what you grow up as, not merely what you are born with." The environmentalists declared that slums produce children with more limited intelligence than generous suburbs do. Not so, asserted the genetically persuaded; poor performance in intellectual matters is the result of a shallow gene-pool.

And so the argument continues. In this past winter's issue of the *Harvard Educational Review*, Dr. Arthur R. Jensen, professor of educational psychology at the University of California at Berkeley, suggests that intelligence is a trait not unlike eye color and hardly more susceptible to change. This study presents an interesting renewal of the genetic argument. Although many of the ideas defended have the aura of statistical, scientific work, they are neither new, self-evident, nor irrefutable. The fact that Dr. Jensen's findings are corroborated by statistical evidence does not make them true. It makes them misleading.

His central thesis is simple: Intelligence is a natural trait, inscribed in the genetic pool and unequally distributed among individuals. Theoretically, genius can be found anywhere, regardless of race or social milieu. In practice, however, Jensen insists that in terms of the average IQ, whites are more intelligent than blacks. The average IQ for blacks is, according to his calculation, approximately 15 points below the average for whites. Furthermore, only 15 per cent of the Negro population exceeds the white average. This has been shown, for instance, in a study (cited by Jensen) by Dr. A. M. Shuey, author of *The Testing of Negro Intelligence*, who reviewed 382 previous studies of IQ. Here we have a typical case of validation by quantification. It is impressive, precise, and wrongheaded. The difference in intelligence between whites and blacks is also noticeable among privileged children; upper-status Negro children average 2.6 IQ points below the low-status whites. Jensen makes the further assertion that Indians, who are even more disadvantaged than Negroes, are nevertheless more intelligent. Jensen is very cautious about this differential intelligence. Negro infants, he claims, are more precocious in sensory-motor development in their first year or two than are Caucasian infants. The same holds for motor skills. But, he believes, what is

SATURDAY REVIEW, May 17, 1969, pp. 73-75 ff.

crucially missing among Negroes is what constitutes genuine formal intelligence: conceptual learning and problem-solving ability.

Jensen offers a description of the respective roles of genetic and environmental factors as he defines intelligence. His strategy in demonstrating the roles of inheritance and environment is to utilize exclusively statistical evidence. He discusses extensively the notion of "heritability," which for him is a statistical mean allowing him to state the extent to which individual differences in a trait such as intelligence can be accounted for by genetic factors. He comes to the conclusion that this heritability is quite high in the human species, which means that genetic factors are much more important than environmental factors in producing IQ differences. And *this* relationship is almost entirely displayed in achievement on IQ tests which Jensen sees as related to genetic differences.

THESE analyses lead Jensen to the further conclusion that genetic factors are strongly implicated in the average Negro-white intelligence differences. Given these conclusions, Jensen ascribes the failure of compensatory education and other educational enrichment programs to genetic differences, because any attempt to raise intelligence per se probably lies more in the province of the biological sciences than in that of psychology and education. For example, the magnitude of IQ and scholastic achievement gains resulting from enrichment and cognitive stimulation programs range between 5 and 20 IQ points. But Jensen is inclined to doubt "that IQ gains up to 8 to 10 points in young disadvantaged children have much of anything to do with changes in ability. They are largely the result of getting a more accurate IQ by testing under more optimal conditions."

Nevertheless, Jensen has some positive recommendations. He distinguishes between two genotypically distinct processes underlying a continuum ranging from "simple" associative learning which he calls Level I, to complex conceptual learning which he calls Level II. Level I involves a relatively high correspondence between the stimulus input and the form of the stimulus output. For example, a child will be able to recite, and perhaps remember, a succession of numbers. Object memory, serial rote learning, and selective trial and error learning are other good examples of Level I. In Level II, a child will be able to classify objects according to their similarities. Thus, Level II involves transforming a stimulus before it becomes an overt response. Concept learning and problem-solving in a whole range of experiences are good examples of Level II. Jensen believes that schooling maximizes the importance of Level II. But schools must also be able to find ways of utilizing other strengths in children whose abilities are not of the conceptual variety. In other words, the ideal educational world of Dr. Jensen would provide two types of education: one directed toward the acquisition of basic skills and simple associative learning, which is training rather than education. Given such training, children with only Level I skills will "perfectly" adapt to any society.

Such is Jensen's thesis. It is based mainly upon the validity of IQ tests. What, in fact, do they measure? The crucial question which must be asked concerns the value of IQ tests themselves. Not that Jensen does not discuss their value. He defines intelligence too narrowly as what IQ tests measure: "a capacity for abstract reasoning and problem-solving." How should we define intelligence? Is it useful to define it at all? In short, the very basis of Jensen's findings must be questioned in the light of what experimental psychology can tell us today about the nature of cognitive development and operations.

For example, fifty years ago any textbook of biology would begin by giving a definition of the word "life." Today, such a procedure is not possible because a definition of life is never adequate. The reason probably lies in the dynamic aspects of the concept, which is incompatible with a static and fixed definition. In a like manner, IQ tests essentially quantify static definitions. Therefore, as in biology it is no longer possible to define life statically, so, too, in psychology a static definition of intelligence is impossible. To understand the limitations of Jensen's basic assumptions, it is helpful to consider the point of view of the Swiss psychologist, Dr. Jean Piaget. A brief summary of the Piagetian approach allows us to differentiate between what is measured by standard intelligence tests and what is discovered through the Piagetian technique.

During more than forty years of experimentation, Dr. Piaget has arrived at a formal description of cognitive development and has divided it into four stages. The first one, before the development of language (symbolic function) in the child, deals with the construction of the logic of actions. This has been called "the period of sensory-motor intelligence." Primarily, the process involves the organization of actions into operational patterns, or "schemata of actions," whose main characteristics are to allow the child to differentiate in his actions, between means and goals. Some conditions are necessary in order to achieve this: Space must become organized as a general container; objects must remain permanent; and, in order to anticipate goals, one must assume some acquisition of practical causal processes.

THE main consequence of the appearance of the symbolic function is the reorganization of sensory-motor intelligence. This enables the child to integrate symbols, allowing him to expand the range of his operations. This next stage is called "pre-operational," or "the period of egocentric thinking." Thus, from a response to an event, intelligence is mediated through language, but the child is not yet able to maintain in his mind symbols (abstractions) that lead to ideas whose meanings are constant. Those constancies have to do with those aspects of the "real world," such as measure, mass, motion, and logical categories. In this pre-operational world everything appears to be related to an egocentric point of view. This is a limitation as much as a source of enrichment during this level of intellectual functioning.

The following stage is characterized by the development of concrete operations. From what is essentially a subjective orientation, intellectual functioning moves toward more objectivity in elaborating mental constancies. The child no longer thinks only in terms of himself, but also takes into account the limitations that the external, physical world places upon him. For example, the child no longer believes that the moon follows him down the street. For Piaget, this type of intelligence is called "concrete," because essentially the child is only able to deal with tangible, manipulatable objects. That is, his world is concerned with *necessary* relations among objects.

The final stage of intellectual development deals with the development of formal thinking which permits the formation not only of necessary relations but also *possible* and *impossible* ones. In short, he can "play" with his mind. The child, now an adolescent, can dream things that never were and ask "Why not?" The adolescent is able to make exact deductions, to extract all combinations from a potential or a real situation. He is no longer directed only by concrete relations. He can make hypotheses and elaborate theories. He is able to dissociate the form of his thinking from its content.

Piaget's approach strongly contrasts with Jensen's point of view. In particular, Piagetian "tests" clearly differ from typical IQ tests. Among the major differences, IQ tests are essentially an additive progression of acquired skills. They give a state, a global or overall result for a specific population; their quantitative aspect allows one to place a child among children of his age and development. Piagetian tests, on the other hand, are hierarchical; they describe a progressive organization and individual potentialities. They provide a detailed analysis of the functioning of thinking. In short, they qualify thinking; they do not quantify it. They always respect the intelligence of a specific child.

These differences are important because, given Piaget's theory, we can describe intelligence functionally; we can formalize its structural development. We cannot assign to intelligence a specific, static definition, in terms of properties, for this directly contradicts the idea of development itself. Any static definition reduces intelligence either to exclusively environmental factors or to almost exclusively genetic factors without implying the necessary *equilibrated* interaction between them.

Consider the distinction between Level I and Level II as proposed by Jensen. At first glance, this argument is appealing; transformations are not involved in the process of decoding and understanding information at Level I, whereas transformations are a necessity at Level II.

But what is a transformation? In a fundamental sense, the understanding of *any* transformation is a necessity at both levels of learning. Without distinguishing a transformation in the real world, we would be unable to differentiate one state from another. For instance, we can present to a child glass A of particular width and height and glass B thinner but taller than A. We call the state in which A is filled up and B is empty S-1, and the state in which B is filled and A is empty S-2. We call transformations (T) the pathway from one state to another, that is, in this particular case, the pouring from A to B, as well as the change of level in S-2 since the level of the liquid is higher than in S-1. For the child to understand these two aspects of the transformation, he must be able to understand the operation of conservation because it is this operation which has produced the transformation from one state to another. In other words, the child "makes the discovery" that the amount of water in the short, fat glass is exactly the same when it is poured into the tall, thin glass. Knowledge of the states themselves, however, is only a description of the observable. This point is fundamental. The fact that conservation is achieved by a child around the age of six or seven clearly implies the necessity of mastering invariancies even in order to understand Level I. But, to grasp any invariancy requires the ability to think, even at a very low level, in operational terms.

Thus, the two levels proposed by Jensen are inadequate to provide a clear idea of the development of intelligence itself.

Piaget, on the other hand, never gives a static definition of intelligence; essentially, he gives a functional one. The two functions of intelligence are to understand the external world and to build or discover new structures within it. Therefore, Piaget's experiments would always be culture-fair, because they are involved with a description of a progressive organization directed by logic and not greatly influenced by culture. For example, a whole set of Piagetian experiments have been carried out in Africa, Algeria, Iran, and elsewhere. *The main result is that sequential development, in comparable terms, is observed irrespective of the culture or the race.* In other words, the stages are respected in their succession and do not permit, even in a theoretical continuum, division into the type of level differences that Jensen describes, and they most strongly suggest the irrelevance of these genotypically distinct basic processes.

IN contrast, IQ tests have been designed by whites for Western culture.

Thus, their value is limited to the culture within which they were designed. They can never be culture-fair. Therefore, in any testing procedure of intelligence, relativity, not absolutism, should be the criterion, and even the correction of IQ tests for other populations is not valid. Furthermore, IQ tests are simply not adequate to measure processes of thinking. They provide results, they do not lead to an understanding of how intelligence functions. Piaget's approach not only allows an understanding of intellectual functioning but describes it. Furthermore, Piaget's tests allow one to make reliable, individual prognostications. Since their interests lie in a description of the mechanism of thinking, they permit an individual, personalized appraisal of further potentialities independent of the culture. This point is important primarily because it is neglected in IQ tests where the global population is assessed rather than individual potentialities estimated.

If one accepts the premises on which IQ tests are based, then Jensen's point of view could be valid for what concerns the differences in Negro-white performances, and nevertheless remain questionable for ethnic differences based on genetic facts. His approach produces logical fallacies: first, he criticizes and compares the results of IQ tests; next, given differences, he sorts out the environmental and genetic factors; then he minimizes the influence of the milieu, analyzes the remainder in terms of biological implications, and finally compares two ethnic groups and ascribes their differences to genetic factors.

Although Jensen's methodology may have its merits, the problem is that the point of departure is wrong. To decide whether compensatory and other educational programs are failures is an important and responsible act. But, to base a judgment on IQ gains or lack of gains is questionable. Of course, one must have a way to judge such programs. But to decide that the IQ gains are so small that they do not justify the amount of money poured into such educational enterprises, can give people the impression that psychologists and educators know what they are talking about concerning processes of learning. In reality, many factors make it difficult to assess success and failure in educational programs. Of course, any program must be globally appraised and must work for a reasonably large number of children. But one of the problems of education is that very little is known about the underlying processes of learning. *Futhermore, pedagogy provides generalized techniques for what must be individualized teaching.* Not much is known about how the child grasps and achieves important notions such as conservation, seriation, number, movement, mass, motion, measure, speed, time, and logical categories. This is true regardless of race, color, or creed. Judging educational programs in terms of IQ does not settle the learning problem. On the contrary, psychologists who place their confidence in IQ tests tend to forget the real issue, which is the critical problem of how the child learns.

The tragedy of education lies in the fact that we are still lacking knowledge about learning processes. This situation should make us modest, and we should accept the fact that the nature of cognitive learning remains an open question for experimental and developmental psychology.

One of the major aims in education is to create openness to cognitive contradictions. One does not learn without confusion. One does not learn without feeling some discrepancy between the actual outlook and an imaginable one. One of the major conditions for cognitive development is the resolution of conflicts which leads to adaptation. Therefore, when Jensen states that we should let those who cannot attain his second level of intellectual functioning develop their capabilities within the limitations of his Level I, his position is a dangerous one strictly on cognitive grounds. It prescribes a limitation on experience for the four- or five-year-old who already has an egocentric view of his world. If learning is to take place in the often confusing circumstances of childhood, then the purpose of teaching is precisely to exploit such circumstances, not to limit them.

Briefly stated, the process of cognitive development in logico-mathematical knowledge is a gradual structuring from inside the child rather than a generalization from repeated external events. Dr. C. Kamii from the Ypsilanti Public Schools makes the point relative to her experience in teaching, following Piaget's model, that if we really want children to learn it is the *process* of interacting with the environment which must be emphasized rather than a specific response already decided upon by the teacher. This idea of process is never considered in Jensen's approach to the problem, either in his theoretical position or in his pedagogical evaluation. In Piaget's conception of process, the idea of emphasizing logical conflicts is naturally involved. Jensen's view of process excludes it.

A primary role of the teacher is to be able to follow the process and to provide creative conflicts at appropriate moments. In the long run, the imposition of rules is a less efficient way to teach than influencing the development of underlying cognitive processes that will eventually enable the child to construct his own rules, which will square with physical reality. Thus, teaching must provide methods whereby the child can make his own discoveries. As stated by the Harvard psychologist, Dr. Lawrence Kohlberg, the cognitive developmental view of teaching aims at building broad, irreversible structures rather than the achievement of immediate gains which may be short-term. Immediate gains, and very specific abilities, measured through IQ increments seem to be the only concern of Jensen. But as Piaget states: "The goal in education is not to increase the amount of knowledge, but to create possibilities for a child to invent and discover. . . . When we teach too fast, we keep the child from inventing and discovering himself. Teaching means creating situations where structures can be discovered; it does not mean transmitting structures which may be assimilated at nothing other than a verbal level."

The whole creative aspect of learning and teaching is completely lost in Jensen's point of view. The child is reduced to a ratio. The teaching act becomes a mechanical adjustment of narrowly identified capacities to severely limited learning goals. Education must be more generous than this.

Open v. Closed Classrooms

By MARIO D. FANTINI

WE HEAR A GREAT DEAL these days about the open v. the closed society. In the one camp we have the totalitarian social order, referred to as a "closed" society, wherein individuals are actually subservient to the state. In the other camp we have those societies which value the individual over the state and are referred to as "open" societies. It is said further that in one society the individual is "free"; in the other, that he is not.

The seriousness of the conflict between open and closed societies cannot be slighted because both societies are willing to preserve their prized values even at the expense of an all-out war. Consequently, we are talking about very important concepts. Moreover, there is a parallel between societies and the classrooms in which teachers find themselves. There are also open and closed classrooms, which, in a sense, are miniatures of open and closed societies.

If you were to view the schools in this light, you might examine a classroom and see the teacher in the front of the room talking to the class. The class might be listening and taking notes; if an assignment were being made, the students might be writing down the assignment, after which perhaps certain students might ask questions. Soon the class is over and a new class comes in. The teacher again asks for the homework assignments from the previous day, goes on to some new work, dictates some important facts, asks a few questions on the work which should have been prepared for the day, makes an assignment for the following day, and answers some last-minute questions. Then a new group comes in and this pattern is repeated.

You might then examine another room

THE CLEARING HOUSE, October, 1962, vol. 37, 67-71.

where the teacher is, at first, hard to find. She is in the background, but the students are moving around freely. Various projects are being undertaken by small groups of students, while other students are working alone. In this classroom, there does not seem to be a routinized approach.

In a sense, you could say that these were observations of open and closed classrooms. In the foregoing descriptions, the first exemplified a closed classroom, while the second one approached the open classroom.

It is my assumption that both classrooms are miniature social systems, in which certain values are being developed (whether the teacher realizes it or not) because of the kind of conditions which the teacher has set up. It is my further assumption that the values sponsored by these miniature social systems parallel many of the values which underline the open and closed societies. It is my belief, also, that there are in operation more of the closed classroom systems than the open classroom systems. If these assumptions are valid, then a possible conclusion is that our schools are actually developing more closed society values than open. This means that American schools are preparing individuals for a closed society, when it is obvious that the schools should be doing just the opposite.

Why do we seem to have more closed than open classrooms? For one reason, the closed system seems to be much more systematic. It appears to be more logical. Since we seem to have inherited this pattern, this seems to be the "way to do it"; so this structure is perpetuated. Since in the closed classroom system the teacher is the center of attraction, this becomes a teachercentric type of arrangement. The individuals, the learners, take their signals largely from the teacher. You can compare this with the closed society, in which the individual takes his signals from the state. Thus, the model projected here is one based on the assign-recite-test sequence. This is the normal methodology. Conformity is being fostered because of the teacher-ascribed standards, which are supposedly sanctioned as being objective. The individual here is in competition with others. The climate fostered here is one in which the prize is on convergent values. The individual must conform or he does not succeed. These convergent values breed conformity, so that ultimately you have a miniature conforming classroom society.

In a closed classroom, such student questions as these are typical: "How long do you want this assignment?" "May we use other textbooks?" "Do you want a bibliography?" The emphasis on these questions is to get permission from the teacher in order to proceed. The teacher is the source of "truth." As long as one goes along with the values and standards that the teacher has imposed, he will gain status and recognition and thereby succeed. The ironic aspect here is that we are making conformists of bright students, those very students who may be called upon to give us the creative leadership we need on a national level. Some students do rebel against the system. These become "outsiders" and usually fail. Most learners conform to the system and, in the process of conforming, internalize these convergent values which, in turn, become an excellent orientation for participation in a closed society.

Moreover, in the closed system the important thing is to *acquire knowledge*—that is, you must know *about* subject matter. The knowing about subject matter is what will be tested, and if the recall is good, the learner will be rewarded. The entire approach in the closed classroom is deductive; the *answers* are more important than the *process* for achieving answers. In all probability, facts will be emphasized at the expense of the conceptual structure. The school administration seems to be satisfied with this operation because it creates little organizational conflict. Parents do not object since this is the same pattern to which they themselves were exposed.

97

The open classroom, on the other hand, is a replica of an open society and, hopefully, can develop those values needed to support and advance an open society—that is, freedom with self-direction. In the open classroom the teacher is largely in the background and the situation is one in which the pupils are the center of attraction. This is the pupilcentric structure. The important value which is developed here is creative self-expression. Just as the center of the open society is the individual and not the state, the center of the open classroom is the student and not the teacher. The climate being fostered is one which permits the development of the creative person and the inner-directed person (to use Riesman's term), since the individual takes his signals from within himself. He is competing with himself, and not with others, so that standards are actually relative to the individual. Critical thinking is being fostered because the process here is *inductive*. It is a search. It is the process of exploration. The answer is not given first; rather, the learner must attempt to discover new ideas and new concepts which will give meaning to further performance.

In the open classroom, the process is valued as much as the product. Further, the open classroom is more prone to be action oriented than is the closed system, where the learner is passive and the teacher is the dominant force. The open classroom swings the emphasis from teaching to learning, to those conditions which surround learning for each student.

If you were able to move through the school systems in our country, you would not find it difficult to determine whether the emphasis is more on the open or closed classroom systems. Certainly, there are values to both, but this is not the major point that is being discussed here. What is being suggested is that an important relationship exists between the classroom and society. Ultimately, what is being learned in the classroom should prepare individuals for competent societal roles. The values of freedom, creativity, and self-direction, so basic to our society, do not just happen. They are developed, and the classroom is one of the important laboratories in the process. Not being cognizant of the values being developed in the classroom is to damage the foundations of a free society. The emphasis today in a free society is on the development of creative individuals. Everyone has the potential for creativity and everyone has a potential for excellence in some area of human endeavor. Each person is born with a particular set of abilities which can be developed to the fullest if the school would provide favorable conditions which foster this development. The emphasis on the creative individual, it seems to me, is founded on an important philosophical position which states that in our type of civilization, the dignity and worth of the individual are supreme. Under this concept, the individual, because of his uniqueness, has the ability to express himself in a unique way. The fruits of his uniqueness can lead to creative expression, whether it be in music, in dance, or in play-acting. This development, it seems to me, is more likely to find expression in the open classroom environment.

If you stand apart to view the educational process as it takes place in the schools, you can see a kind of continuum from the open to the closed system. It is surprising how we begin our education with an open system and gradually proceed to a more closed type of classroom system. For example, the kindergarten is an excellent model of the open classroom, but as we move through the grades the situation changes. What we are doing actually, instead of nurturing creativity, is creating conditions that stymie creative growth.

However, the open system is not a panacea and there are certain important arguments against the open classroom systems. The first is that it is difficult for a teacher to control an open system—that it lacks discipline—that there is a lack of teacher control. The argument continues that in the absence of someone in charge in the room, utter chaos would follow. For example, it is often cited that the teacher who is weak and does not have authority is subjected to behavior abuses because of lack of control.

My answer to this argument would be that in an open society, the highest form of discipline is not imposed discipline but self-discipline; i.e., the internalization of a certain set of values which give meaning and purpose to behavior. This is the sought-for kind of ideal. If this is not true, then the argument is really in favor of a nation of followers. One of the most severe criticisms of our times is that we have become a nation of conformists. If you were to look back in time, a counter argument could be raised, based on the school years; i.e., retracing the causes of conformity could lead logically to the classroom and to the lack of sufficient opportunities to exercise and to internalize types of behavior patterns which would develop self-direction. Consequently, since the development of self-discipline is inherent in the open system, its practice should be encouraged. Conversely, the closed system is more likely to sponsor the other-directed orientation.

Another argument that is often cited is that the open system is one that is more apt not to cover the subject matter that needs to be covered. The knowledge which we should be giving to the students would not be taught under an open system. The argument continues that it is important to outline the course work in a logical fashion and to cover a certain amount of work each day so that, over a period of time, the essentials are covered.

However, if you examine knowledge today, you realize that it is expanding at a geometric rate. It is impossible to expect one person to know all. Moreover, the nature of knowledge is changing. The orientation of many teachers took place at a time when knowledge was not expanding at a geometric rate, and there is no guarantee that the teacher has kept up with changing perspectives in his own discipline. Consequently, it is not knowledge that is important, but the ideas and concepts which underly the change in the framework of knowledge. This is the very thing that an open classroom seeks—to give the person, through the process of inquiry, the method for discovering the big ideas which have given meaning to change. In addition, those who would argue that knowledge would be neglected under an open system, at the same time underestimate value development. The open classroom system stimulates the process for development of such values as freedom, critical thinking, self-direction, creativity, and cooperation—those very values which give meaning and direction to democratic functioning. Students in this open system are experiencing patterns of behavior which are more like the ideals of the open and free society in which they will eventually become members.

An argument often cited against closed systems is that the closed system is more prone to developing a passive individual. Since the teacher is the center of dominance in the closed system, the student's role is primarily passive. The student is the recipient of a flow of communication from the teacher. By contrast, the learner in the open system is quite active because he must go through the process of exploring and discovering. Moreover, this active process, encouraged by the open system, serves also to fortify the learner with a particular method for discovering answers to problems, which is based on a major tool of science—the scientific method. The breakthroughs which we have in the field of science are largely attributable to increased sophistication in the implementation of this method. Actually, an open classroom is fortifying the learner with tools for problem solving in an age when it is necessary for a person to be able to think through the complexities of modern life to the degree, at least, of gaining insights which would enable him to recognize the significant from the insignificant. These are all attributes which are possible of development in a classroom which takes on the characteristics more of an open than of a closed system.

The question arises, "Why are there not more open than closed classroom systems?" This is, again, a complex problem. One answer is that this would necessitate a new orientation for most teachers. It is actually a much more difficult challenge to create the learning environment of an open classroom. For example, as a new teacher moves into the school situation, he becomes a member of a social system. He usually is not in a position to initiate change, and must go along with the norms of the system. The process of shifting a classroom situation from a closed to an open one is often fraught with hazards for the beginner. It may be that over a period of time the beginner succumbs to the pressures of the system. More likely, however, the closed system is found to be the easier way out. The closed system seems to be more definite. The teacher sees the logic of the approach more readily. He feels more satisfaction in having covered a given body of subject matter and in testing the student to see what he has learned. He seems to get more reward out of knowing his place in teaching.

The open system, on the other hand, is difficult to assess in terms of the teacher's role. The teacher in the open system is more of a climate setter, one who, while remaining in the background, is actually the agent who brings into the classroom environment all of the resources which implement learning.

Whether we realize it or not, education is playing a vital role in terms of national purpose. We are getting an awakening of the importance of education in the total process of developing an ideal type of society. Sooner or later we must come to the conclusion that schools have specific and major functions in society, and that this function concerns itself mainly with socializing all the citizens to perform effectively and maturely in the society in which they will function. That is, the school should attempt to develop the individual to the fullest, because, as a self-realizing individual, he will best make a contribution to the development of a free and open civilization.

Certainly, we are hopeful that the schools will develop the kind of individual who has social responsibility, one who feels deeply for humanity. In order to develop the kind of individual called for in this type of free order, the schools have a vital role to perform.

As we examine the educational process closely, it becomes apparent that serious consideration should be given to the nature of the teaching front, to that environmental situation in which teaching and learning take place. Hopefully, that direction will be more toward the model of the open classroom system.

The Textbook— Procrustean Bed of Learning

By FENWICK ENGLISH

ONE of the cherished and hallowed idols of public education is at last exhibiting signs of decay and falling into well-earned disrepute: the textbook. For generations it has been the Procrustean bed to which we have subjected students. Like Procrustes, we have either stretched our students' legs or cut them off to fit the textbook.

According to *The Rand McNally Handbook on Education*,[1] "The role of the textbook in instruction is a major issue in education." The handbook also noted that as late as 1956 "textbooks continued to be the core of instructional materials in this country." The trend away from the textbook began with three contemporary phenomena, which I shall discuss.

It has been estimated by Claude Fawcett[2] that it takes 10 years for a textbook to be born. This would include the writing, editing, adopting, printing, evaluating, purchasing, and distributing. Glass says of our newest science textbooks that they will be out of date, like a new car, in five years and need revision.[3] We are all familiar with the fact that because of the pace of our modern industrial and technological society, we are roughly doubling man's accumulated store of knowledge each decade.

In California $9 to $15 million was spent last year, according to Caspar Weinberger,[4] to prepare outdated, and in some instances, false information for students to learn as established truth because the "text says so." As students, we may remember physics books which showed the atom as a permanent structure. We memorized this structure as immutable fact. Today it is a false picture of the nature of the atom. Thus it is not only impossible for a textbook to be contemporary, but equally impossible for it to be authoritative.

Any book which after the time it is published and placed in the hands of students fails to include half of man's total experience in that field cannot be authoritative.

The problem of increasing knowledge and the inability of traditional texts in coping with it has been highlighted by Lawrence Metcalf.[5] In the area of history the buildup of detail has led to the practice of "easy familiarity." This is the result of having more and more to say in about the same space of previous textbooks. Metcalf summarizes that "the only solution is for the writer to express himself in generalities, leaving out the detail that would give these generalities meaning." Metcalf reiterates William James' law that "no one sees any

PHI DELTA KAPPAN, 1967, Vol. 48, pp. 393-395.

101

further into a generalization than his knowledge of detail extends."

Whitehead[6] dealt with such hollow generalizations as "inert ideas," that is, ideas learned "without being utilized or tested, or thrown into fresh combinations." The "facts" or "concepts" of the text learned in the abstract can only be remembered in the abstract. This is what makes the practice of cramming inevitable, and the loss of that information equally inevitable. The lack of application or rigorous examination of text concepts deludes students into thinking they may really understand something when the text is "merely clever in its language and phrasing."[7]

Research and investigation into the nature of learning have revealed many fallacies upon which previous assumptions about learning have been based. One of these identified by Walker[8] is the "whole class concept of teaching." Walker explains that this is the notion that "groups of 30 or more students are expected to learn the same thing at the same time and at approximately the same speed."

Richard Suchman[9] has attacked this concept on the following basis. "Any teacher who takes the time to determine the level of conceptual readiness and intrinsic motivation of each of his pupils before and during his teaching activities finds that it makes no sense to teach an entire group of children as a group. He can never presume that any two children start from the same set of concepts and move with equal speed and along parallel lines of conceptual growth."

Because the textbook is based upon the "whole-class concept" and the idea that all students will begin and end at the same point, it confines students to one level. It acts as the Procrustean bed. By narrowing thinking and learning to this level it bores the student who wishes to forge ahead, and leaves behind those with little interest, read-

ing difficulties, or the inability to pursue further study. It is the result of the idea of "gradedness."

Many teachers rely upon the textbook as the authoritarian block upon which to chop off student inquiry. A teacher who hides between the covers of the text finds safety by confining learning to within its scope. In this way it is very easy to conceal one's own ignorance; it is a tacit refusal to keep abreast of the times. Student learning is similarly confined, if we can believe the notion that effective instruction increases the differences and levels of achievement of the learners.

Ben Bloom[10] has illustrated that cognition occurs on many levels. If we apply his *Taxonomy of Educational Objectives* as a criterion to judge the caliber of typical questions at the end of a chapter, we find that few, if any, are outside of category one, or "the recall of specific facts, principles, classifications, and categories." When a student answers a question involving who, what, when, or where, and copies directly from a passage in the preceding chapter, it is possible for him to have a correct answer without comprehending the meaning of the answer. Thus Bloom's cognitive category of "comprehending" is only rarely touched. It is usually the case that no question enters into the higher levels identified in the *Taxonomy*, such as analysis, application, synthesis, or evaluation. If most of our classroom time is spent in having students regurgitate items in Bloom's area one, we have tapped only the most shallow and superficial of human mental talents: the ability to memorize. Memorization does not necessarily include understanding or the ability to apply information or learned skills to a problem; in short, the questions at the chapter's end are too often examples of "inert ideas." William Burton[11] has labeled a parallel practice of the page assignment in a single text followed by a formal verbal quiz as "grossly ineffective" and "calculated to interfere with learning."

An equally absurd idea that many teachers and administrators fret over is the idea that one must be sure and "cover" the text content within a given period of time. We have shown that no two children ever begin together in even one dimension of learning, let's say the quality and quantity of information acquired. What we really mean by "cover" is that the teacher exposes the group to a certain sequence of ideas, continuity of material, lists of categories, etc. The assumption expressed in this idea is that a given amount of exposure equals a given amount of learning. But we all know better.

A half-century ago John Dewey[12] challenged the continuity notion when he said, "The most scientific matter arranged in most logical fashion loses this quality, when presented in external, ready-made fashion, by the time it gets to the child. It has to undergo some modification in order to shut out some phases too hard to grasp, and to reduce some of the attendant difficulties. What happens? Those things which are most significant to the scientific man, and most valuable in the logic of actual inquiry and classification, drop out. The really thought-provoking character is obscured, and the organizing function disappears. . . . So the subject matter is evacuated of its logical value, and, though it is what it is only from the logical standpoint, is presented as stuff only for 'memory.' "

Further examination of text questions will reveal the degree to which they demand the convergent type of thinking to arrive at the "right" answer. Hilda Taba[13] has labeled such "right" answers as those depending on "authority rather than on rational judgment." Taba's remarks, while directed toward the teacher, take the textbook into account for producing acts which "control and limit the responses of students and thereby inhibit their mental activity beyond that which is necessary for orderly development of thought."

The textbook has reduced student interests and abilities to one level. It has promoted mediocrity, apathy, and the continuance of generations of passive learners. The exercises, questions, drills, etc., center primarily on convergent answer-giving behavior. Rarely are students challenged by textbooks to produce divergent, creative acts or perform analysis on the logic of the ideas or organization of the content. Research on cognition and the need to produce and accentuate differences have relegated the textbook to the era of the hornbook and the duncecap. It is a relic in the educational museum of obsolescence.

The impact of instructional technology and the systems approach to education have also imperiled the textbook's future. A. A. Lumsdaine[14] revealed the epitome of the highly analytical approach in his definition of the word instruction, "a generic term referring to any specificable means of controlling or manipulating a sequence of events to produce modifications of behavior through learning. It is applicable whenever the outcomes of learning can be specified in sufficiently explicit terms to permit their measurement. These outcomes may include changes in attitudes, interests, motivations, beliefs, or opinions as well as in knowledges, skills, and other performance capabilities."

Lumsdaine drops the textbook as a valid instructional material because "The usual textbook does not control behavior of the learner in a way which makes it highly predictable as a vehicle of instruction or amenable to experimental research. It does not in itself generate a describable and predictable process of learner behavior.

. . ." The textbook will eventually be replaced by programmed materials and a new array of factual handbooks.

Virgil Herrick[15] has succinctly stated the limitations of the textbook as an instructional aid. Paraphrased arguments are:

1. The textbook cannot think or discover. This has to be done by the student.

2. The textbook should not be the sole instrument for organizing and developing the major ideas, or for relating this pattern of ideas to the problems and experiences of a particular group of students.

3. The textbook should not be the sole determinant of what is to be taught.

4. A textbook cannot determine the speed with which a student moves through his learning activities or the speed with which they move past him. A textbook can do very little to help a child pace his learning according to his purpose and the nature of the content being studied.

5. Learning, if it is to be valuable, must be evaluated and then applied to future learning and behavior. A textbook has very little to do with this problem.

In summary, the textbook in its present form is outdated, expensive, and inefficient. The assumptions underlying its present usage are false; they do not explain or foster learning in depth or promote student inquiry. Educators must now begin the task of informing the public and lobbying for a change in state textbook laws which require "uniform use" of texts provided free by the state. The removal of legal straitjackets will provide the freedom necessary to arrive at modern education in a time when "modern" is woefully out of date.

[1]Arthur W. Foshay (ed.), *Rand McNally Handbook of Education.* Chicago: Rand McNally, 1963.

[2]Claude W. Fawcett, "Technological Change and Education," *Journal of Secondary Education*, January, 1961.

[3]H. Bentley Glass, "What Man Can Be." (Address at the February, 1967, Convention of the American Association of School Administrators, Atlantic City.)

[4]Caspar W. Weinberger, "Lack of Coordination Seems at Root of Textbook Trouble," *Los Angeles Times*, March 30, 1966.

[5]Lawrence E. Metcalf, "Research on Teaching the Social Studies," *Handbook of Research on Teaching*, N. L. Gage (ed.). Chicago: Rand McNally, 1963.

[6]Alfred North Whitehead, *The Aims of Education and Other Essays.* New York: The Macmillan Company, 1929.

[7]Metcalf, *op. cit.*

[8]A. Reed Walker, "Education and Individuality," *The Bulletin of the National Association of Secondary School Principals*, December, 1965.

[9]Richard J. Suchman, "Learning Through Inquiry," *Childhood Education*, February, 1965.

[10]Benjamin S. Bloom, *Taxonomy of Educational Objectives. Handbook I Cognitive Domain.* New York: David McKay Co., 1956.

[11]William H. Burton, "Implications for the Organization of Instruction and Instructional Adjuncts," *Learning and Instruction*, 49th Yearbook of the National Society for the Study of Education. Chicago: University of Chicago Press, 1950.

[12]John Dewey, *The Child and the Curriculum.* Chicago: University of Chicago Press, 1902.

[13]Hilda Taba, "Teaching Strategy and Learning," *California Journal for Instructional Improvement*, VI, No. 4, December, 1963.

[14]A. A. Lumsdaine, "Instruments and Media of Instruction," *A Handbook of Research on Teaching*, N. L. Gage (ed.). Chicago: Rand McNally, 1963.

[15]Virgil E. Herrick, *The Elementary School.* New Jersey: Englewood Cliffs, 1956.

The Language and Values of Programmed Instruction

DONALD G. ARNSTINE

I

IN THE PAST FEW YEARS, the sponsors of teaching machines and programmed instruction have assaulted with increasing vigor the tradition-bound and barnacled bastions of American schools. A great many educators, with cries of "mechanization" and "long live the unprogrammable child," have stood firm at the gates, but the onslaught has not slackened; the issue is still in doubt. It is the aim of this essay to penetrate the camp of the programmers, count their troops, and assess their strength. As yet, the combatants themselves have not done this: the programmers, because their strategy precludes it, and their opponents, because good reasons are not easily found in the heat of combat.

The claims of the champions of programmed instruction are often magnificent and awe-inspiring. Across their banners might be inscribed the words of one of their doughtiest generals: "Once we have specified the behavior [involved in the act of thinking itself] . . . we have no reason to suppose that it will then be any less adaptable to programmed instruction than simple verbal repertoires."[1]

[1] B. F. Skinner, "Why We Need Teaching Machines," *Harvard Educational Review*, 31:4, p. 397

Optimism for the future of programmed instruction is shared by those who develop the programs; thus Harry F. Silberman, of Systems Development Corporation, writes, ". . . any domain of instruction, including creativity, is fair game for programming."[2] Another enthusiast claims that the program duplicates the work of that "superb teaching mechanism," and human tutor: "Those of us who share the enthusiasm for computer-based teaching machines do so because a computer allows us . . . to approach full simulation of the human tutorial process."[3]

Thus it is clear that confidence is not lacking in the camp of the programmers: "It seems perfectly reasonable," writes Lloyd E. Homme, "to say that the machine teaching enterprise cannot fail."[4] Homme then goes on to elaborate his own vision of the schools of tomorrow:

[2] Silberman, "What Are the Limits of Programmed Instruction?" *Phi Delta Kappan*, XLIV:6, p. 296. The answer to the question in Silberman's title: none.
[3] William R. Uttal, "On Conversational Interaction," in John E. Coulson (ed.), *Programmed Learning and Computer-Based Instruction* (New York: John Wiley, 1962), p. 172.
[4] Homm, "The Rationale of Teaching by Skinner's Machines," in A. A. Lumsdaine and Robert Glaser (eds.), *Teaching Machines and Programmed Learning: A Source Book* (Washington, D.C.: Department of Audiovisual Instruction of the NEA, 1960), p. 136.

THE EDUCATIONAL FORUM, Jan. 1964, vol. 28, pp. 219-226.

"In fact, I will go so far as to predict that classrooms of the future, their walls lined with exotic machines, will resemble nothing so much as the emporiums of Las Vegas. I am even willing to bet that the players will be equally intense in their pursuit of reinforcements."[5]

Unchecked, such enthusiasm is a powerful force. This is important because it is not the programmers themselves, but rather school administrators and boards of education who will ultimately make the decisions about whether to use programmed instruction in the schools and, if so, in what kinds of situations to use it. Since decisions of this sort ought not to be made on the basis of persuasive rhetoric or the results of often carelessly designed research studies, it is the aim of the present essay to assist those who would carefully evaluate the contribution of programmed instruction to the enterprise of education in schools.

Empirical research directed at the efficacy of instructional programs provides little guidance for such careful evaluation. Not only is the design of such research often ill-conceived,[6] but the results of that research when applied to

areas within general education are often contradictory when they are not trivial.[7] The discussion that follows, then, will attempt to avoid some of the pitfalls into which empirical investigators have often tripped by examining some of the assumptions that these investigators take for granted *before* conducting their research. Since such an examination is not always a matter of empirical investigation, the focus of the discussion that follows will be on the language and on the implied values on which the theoretical support of programming and the arguments for utilizing programming in schools are predicated.

The phrase "programmed instruction" will be used to refer to any instruction presented by means of a program, and a program "is designed to present material to the learner and to control the student's behavior during his learning by exposing stimulus material, requiring some overt or covert response to this material and providing some form of knowledge of results for each response. It is a program in the sense that it is a list of items, steps, or frames, each of which performs these functions."[8] A "teaching machine" is any device, mechanical or electronic, designed to present the program and facilitate the learner's response to it.

In the subsequent discussion, remarks will be directed to the program, not the

[5] *Ibid.* Other equally sanguine prognostications will be found in Simon Ramo, "A New Technique of Education," *Engineering and Science Monthly*, 21, pp. 17-22, and in James D. Finn, "Automation and Instruction: III, Technology and the Instructional Process," *A V Communication Review*, 8:1, pp. 5-26.

[6] James G. Holland states, "Aside from the over-generalization inevitable from . . . ill-defined variables [selected in research studies], even these relatively uninteresting problems are inadequately treated. Despite the overwhelming recognition of the importance of quality in the program, we are seldom given information for evaluating the program." (New Directions in Teaching Machine Research," in Coulson, *op. cit.*, p. 47.)

[7] See, for example, Lawrence M. Stolurow, *Teaching by Machine* (Washington, D.C.: U.S. Government Printing Office, 1961), Chapter VII.

[8] Joseph W. Rigney and Edward B. Fry, "Programming Techniques," *A V Communication Review*, 9:5, p. 7.

machine, since the machine is only a means for presenting the program to the student. Besides, research has found the program to be equally effective with or without the machine.[9] In order, then, to meet the defense that today's machines are certain to undergo subsequent refinement and improvement, we shall focus on the *program* and assume the possible existence of a computer-based machine of any desired complexity that will present the program to students. Thus the following remarks are not to be considered as limited by present inadequacies of teaching machines.

The analysis of programmed instruction must proceed on two fronts: 1) is the theory of teaching exemplified by programming tenable? and 2) what will be the results of various uses of programming in schools, and are these results desirable?

To judge the desirability of programming for school use, both questions must be considered independently. An affirmative answer to the first question (the theory of teaching *is* tenable) does not preclude rejecting the use of programming in schools on the basis of a negative answer to the second question (the results of using programs in schools are *not* desirable). Conversely, a negative answer to the first question (the theory of teaching is *not* tenable) does not pre-

clude recommending the use of programs in schools on the basis of an affirmative answer to the second question (the results of using programs in schools are desirable on the basis of the empirically *observed results* of their use). These observations serve to indicate that, in the fields of human learning and instruction, there is not yet a necessary connection between theory and practice. Hence an evaluation of one has no necessary implications for the other.

It may be helpful to anticipate, at the outset, some of the conclusions that will be discussed in detail in this essay. In what follows it will be claimed that 1) the so-called principles of programming, allegedly based on reinforcement theory, either suffer from the same defects that have been found in that theory, or bear no relation to the theory at all, and 2) the use of programs in schools, in all but a very few limited applications, leads to results that are incompatible with what has immemorially been called, by both scholars and laymen, education. It is now time to turn to the evidence on which these opinions are based.

II

It is usually claimed that the principles of programming are based on reinforcement theory. Although this theory of behavior and learning will not be called into question here,[10] it stands to

[9] See, for example, Stolurow, "Let's be Informed on Programmed Instruction," *Phi Delta Kappan*, XLIV:6: ". . . there is no objective evidence from research to support the need for a machine to assist student learning. . . . The primary factor that makes instruction effective is the program. . . . Existing programmed materials alone when used in book form will teach as well as when used in a machine." (pp. 255 f)

[10] Standard criticisms of reinforcement theory, succintly put, may be readily found in Harry Harlow, "Mice, Monkeys, Men, and Motives," *Psychological Review*, 60, pp. 23-32 and Donald Snygg, "The Tortuous Path of Learning Theory," *Audio Visual Instruction*, 7:1, pp. 8-12. A criticism of B. F. Skinner's operant conditioning

reason that at best these principles can be no more valid than the theory on which they are based. We shall find, however, that the relation between the principles of programming and reinforcement theory is not nearly so clear as programmers claim. Although there are many lists of "principles" of programming, we will simply select the four that are presented and explained in a demonstration course published by one of the nation's most active programming firms, TMI-Grolier.[11] The four principles, to be discussed below in order, are those of 1) small steps, 2) active responding, 3) immediate confirmation, and 4) self-pacing.

1. The Principle of Small Steps. The substance of this principle is that the material to be taught, once carefully delimited, must be broken down into very minute teaching units (or "frames" in the program), each closely related to the succeeding one, until all the material has been presented. This, presumably, makes it easy (and relatively errorless) for the student to acquire the entire body of material.[12] This principle is surely reminis-

cent of Descartes,[13] but it bears no relation at all to reinforcement theory—although the claim is usually made that it follows from the notion of "shaping" behavior by a process of successive approximations (i.e. small steps).[14]

Whatever reasons may be adduced for granulating the material to be learned into small steps, they have nothing to do with successive approximations. When a dog's behavior is being shaped such that it will eventually touch a doorknob with its nose, only the movements that more closely approximate doorknob-touching are reinforced. Each previous movement in the wrong direction is extinguished (i.e. not repeated) because it is not reinforced. If this chain of successive approximations were to be a model for an instructional program, we should be embarrassed to find ourselves insisting that the student's responses to each item or frame be extinguished as he proceeds to the next item. Hence the student would learn only the *last* frame in the program.

But this bizarre eventuality need not concern us, for successive approximations cannot possibly be a model for the verbal learning fostered by an instructional program. When the dog was trained to touch the doorknob with his nose, only the *last* successful series of responses was the "correct" (i.e. desired by the experimenter) one; had the other responses

version of reinforcement theory, at once remarkably concise and comprehensive, may be found in Noam Chomsky's review of Skinner's *Verbal Behavior*, in *Language*, 35:1, pp. 26-58.

[11] *The Principles of Programmed Learning* (Albuquerque, N.M.: Teaching Machines Incorporated, 1961). This programmed course on programming actually presents five "principles," but the fifth one, the "principle of student testing," is not a principle of teaching or learning at all, but a technique for revising an instructional program. The other four principles discussed below are mentioned by all workers in the field.

[12] Part of the difficulty in putting this principle into practice stems from the fact that it is not altogether clear just what a "step" refers to—whether it be item length, difficulty, sequence, or what. For further discussion on this point, see A. A. Lumsdaine, "Some Issues Concerning

Devices and Programs for Automated Learning," in Lumsdaine and Glaser, *op. cit.*, pp. 517-539.

[13] Especially Rules V and VI in the "Rules for the Direction of the Mind," in E. S. Haldane and G. R. T. Ross (trans.), *The Philosophical Works of Descartes*, I: (New York: Dover, 1955).

[14] See, for example, B. F. Skinner, "Teaching Machines," *Science*, 128, pp. 969-977.

not been extinguished, the dog would still be wandering around the room days later. Training the dog, then, involved the animal's eventual selection of one complex behavior sequence out of an infinitely varied continuous series of movements. But when a human learner responds to an instructional program, nearly *every* response is "correct" (i.e. desired by the programmer); hence nearly every response is reinforced, and hardly any responses are extinguished. If hardly any responses are extinguished, then there is no shaping of behavior; nothing at all is being successively approximated[15] because every bit of behavior is precisely correct.

The reason for the incompatibility of the training program for Rover and the instructional program for the human student is not far to seek: success for the dog means selection from a continuous series of responses; there is no way to achieve success *but* to shape the dog's series of acts. But for the student, success means selection from a *dis*continuous series of (verbal) responses; there is a finite number of discrete responses available from which he must choose. Thus literally to shape his behavior would be absurd.

We will close this discussion with an

[15] If it is claimed that the student is really successively approximating the "content of the course," it must then be asked, what *is* the content of the course? If the answer is: all the frames in the program, then again, nothing is being successively approximated in the Skinnerian sense; rather, the learner is simply gradually assimilating the program. But if the content of the course is called something *other than* all the frames in the program, then it must be asked, why didn't the frames directly present this other something for the student to acquire?

example of genuine shaping of a student's verbal behavior. Suppose we want the student to complete the following statement: "All gases are composed of rapidly moving ————." We want the student to say "molecules." The student says, "air." We say nothing. He says "breezes." We say nothing. He says, "movements." We say, "that's good." He says, "emoluments"; we say, "that's good." He says, "moluments," and we say, "you're doing fine." He says, "monuments." We say nothing. He says, "molly's carts"; we say, "now you're getting on the right track." He says, "molly's cubes"; we say, "you're getting warm." He says, "molecules"; we say, "that's right." The student's behavior has been shaped. Q.E.D.

2. The Principle of Active Responding. According to this principle, the student learns best when he is active. When he is passive, he presumably doesn't learn as efficiently. What is needed to test this principle is some specification of how much activity is desirable, and what kind of activity.

For some time, programmers thought that an overt response to an item, such as the filling-in of a blank, or the pressing of a key (indicating selection of a multiple-choice alternative) was "active" and thereby important for learning. However, recent studies indicate that programs allowing only a covert response, or providing no opportunity for a response at all, are just as effective.[16]

The reason for these negative findings

[16] See John F. Feldhusen, "Taps for Teaching Machines," *Phi Delta Kappan*, XLIV:6, pp. 265-267.

is not far to seek: no one had bothered to define "active." In this respect, the dismal history of "learning by doing" has been repeated. When "learning by doing" was grossly interpreted to mean that children learned *only* when participating in committee work or in construction projects, the absurdity of the notion was clearly seen.[17] By the same token, if "active responses" *means* filling in a blank or pressing a key, this notion, with its arbitrary and restrictive limitation, is equally absurd.

An active response is said to make learning more efficient, but there is no doubt that some people learn efficiently from lectures, broadcasts, books, films, and the like. Have such people been active? Suppose, when they were attending a lecture or reading a book, that they were observed to have been sitting quitely—not even taking notes. They may have been no more "active" than others sitting next to them who did *not* (according to subsequent tests) learn efficiently from the lecture or book. If no *observable* activity was apparent in either the efficient or the inefficient learners, but "activity" is still held to account for better learning, shall we then claim that those who learned efficiently were engaged in some rigorous "mental" activity? If this claim is *allowed,* then the possibility of mental activity would surely weaken the arguments in favor of filling in blanks or punching keys. But if the claim of "mental activity" is *rejected*

as an explanation of observably inactive but efficient learning, then such learning, as it often occurs in response to lectures, films, and books, must remain an anomaly in the light of the principle of active responding.

There is little doubt that learning may occur in some cases when no physical activity is observable, and at other times it may occur under conditions of strenuous and highly articulated physical activity. That the learning of all (or even any particular) verbal materials occurs most efficiently only when the learner completes an unfinished sentence or presses an appropriate key has not been demonstrated. The principle of active responding is no more than a suggestion, and in view of the differences among students, learning materials, and educational objectives, a rather vague one at that.

3. The Principle of Immediate Confirmation. This principle holds that the student learns best when immediately presented with knowledge of the results of his response to an item or frame. If the student makes an error, knowledge of results is not reinforcing and his response, it is said, is extinguished. But if the response is correct, the knowledge of results confirms his judgment and is thus reinforcing. Hence he is likely to repeat that behavior when later presented with the same stimulus situation. (This principle also implies that a program must be written in such a way as to minimize the number of student errors; if this is not done, the student will seldom be reinforced and consequently will learn little.)

The problem with this principle is

[17] For an analysis of a closely related conceptual tangle, see John Hanson, "Learning by Experience," in B. O. Smith and Robert H. Ennis (eds.), *Language and Concepts in Education* (Chicago: Rand McNally, 1961), pp. 1-23.

that we have no way of justifying the claim that immediate confirmation is reinforcing to all students in any given school learning situation. Even in carefully designed experiments in which pigeons peck at keys, reinforcement theory does not allow us to *label* food pellets as reinforcers until *after* the sequence of events that includes repeated behavior and eating of the food. Only empirical observation, then, can tell us whether immediate confirmation is really a "principle" of learning, or just a supposition. And researchers have found that when they themselves correctly filled in the blanks in a program and merely asked the students to read the frames, the students learned no less than a comparable group that filled in the blanks themselves and thus received immediate confirmation of their responses.[18] It has also been observed that regularly repeated immediate confirmations became boring for students (the preposterous term used is "pall effect"), and thus remained reinforcers no longer.[19]

Finally, the principle of immediate confirmation begs the question of motivation. It seems hardly deniable that immediate confirmation will have very different effects on students who are interested in the material to be learned and on students who are not. And that people obviously learn from their mistakes is also contrary to the principle of immediate confirmation; this is the basis for the branching-type programs sponsored by Norman Crowder.[20]

We may conclude by saying that some people, when told to learn some sorts of materials, sometimes learn more efficiently when presented with immediate confirmation of their efforts. But this is all the reliable guidance we can get from the principle of immediate confirmation.

4. The Principle of Self-Pacing. It is claimed in this principle that the student spends as much time with the program as he needs to respond to all the items correctly. This much is clear, just as a student spends as much time with an ordinary textbook as he feels he needs to understand it. That everyone learns at his own rate is an analytic statement (that is, true by definition), or else it would make sense to say, "everyone learns at somebody else's rate," or "he learned faster than he could learn." And to say, "he could have learned more quickly" does not mean that the student didn't learn at his own rate. Rather, it means, "he learned (whatever it was he was supposed to learn) *at his own rate* and was then made to do some other things (e.g. work additional problems, wait for others to catch up, etc.) in a period of time in which it is possible that he could have learned something else about the given subject." Of course, the student *did* learn about *something* else: how it feels to be bored, how to sit still when impatient, how to surreptitiously write notes to classmates, etc.

Self-pacing, then, is not at issue in this principle, because learning is always self-paced. The most elaborate teaching device or the best teacher conceivable can only present a student with a situation

[18] Feldhusen, *op. cit.*
[19] *Ibid.*
[20] See Crowder, "Automatic Tutoring by Intrinsic Programming," in Lumsdaine and Glaser (*op. cit.*), pp. 286-298.

that *might* result in his learning;[21] they cannot insure that he will learn what they want him to learn, and it is literally nonsense to claim that they can get him to learn it any faster than he is able to.

Considered in itself, then, the principle of self-pacing is either obvious or implies an absurdity: that in some situations students do not learn at their own rate. The import of this principle, then, must be found elsewhere—namely, in the claim that time is allowed for the student to respond correctly to all the items in the program. This claim, which is quite different from the claim that the

student learns at his own rate, is undeniably just, However, it is of value to educators only if "responding correctly to all the items" is what we mean by education, learning, or learning a particular subject.

That students must have immediate confirmation of their own written or key-pressed responses to a sequence of gradually changing items in order to learn *efficiently* has been questioned in the foregoing discussion. It is now time to ask whether the elicitation of such behavior from students has anything at all to do with learning and education as those terms have ordinarily been used in connection with what goes on in schools.

[21] The distinction between "intentional" and "success" uses of the verb "to teach" is relevant to this point. See Israel Scheffler, *The Language of Education* (Springfield, Ill.: Charles C Thomas, 1960), pp. 41f.

TO GRADE OR NOT TO GRADE

Frances R. Link

In a free adaptation of Hamlet's "to be or not to be" soliloquy, we might ask: Should parents, children, and teachers continue to bear the pains of the grading system, or should they rise up and end their troubles by abolishing grades?

To grade or not to grade is the proposition before us, but it's not the best question to start with. Before considering it, we ought to ask questions about the grading system. And then we ought to ask questions about the questions we asked. Were they the "right" questions — that is, did they have a real bearing on the purposes of education and the purposes of grading or evaluation, as educators call it?

Asking the right questions

We might begin with this question: Does the grading system that we now have reflect or assume a need for the child and his parents to be informed? If the answer is yes, certain other assumptions follow. We would assume that being informed about everything relevant to the child's growth and development is good, that it is healthy. We would assume that the information resulting from evaluation would be used to "admire" the learner — that is, recognize his worth. We would assume also that the system would enable both the child and his parents to be objective about the child's capabilities, skills, feelings, experiments, and mistakes. Of course, these might be quite false assumptions about our school's reporting system. The reality might be very different.

Next we might ask: Does the evaluation system assume that every child is improvable? If it does, then everyone involved in the system — teacher, child, parent — understands that all students can improve somewhat, even A students. There will be no reason for telling a child at each grading period that he needs to improve, which is what is usually done now. The concept that every learner can improve is easily understood by children, perhaps most readily by A students.

THE PTA MAGAZINE, November 1967, pp. 10-12.

The fact that all students are improvable does not mean that they are perfectible. But neither does it mean that we should destroy the vision or hope of perfection. Parents and teachers often seek or demand perfection in children instead of nurturing the vision. What I would emphasize here is that all students can be better than they are by at least a little bit, that students know this, and that it doesn't have to be hammered home at every reporting period.

Now some further questions: Does our evaluation system assume that the child likes to be justly and fairly appreciated? If we agree that just and fair appreciation is an important human need and that it helps the child want to achieve, then we ought to have a system that communicates appreciation when it is deserved. The current system assumes that the child is deserving at predetermined periods, such as every six weeks or four times a year. The result is that *not deserving* gets the same emphasis as *deserving*. Appreciation, if there is any, is expressed outside the system or happens as a side effect at best. The current system rarely deals realistically with the human need to be appreciated.

Another question to ask is, Does the evaluation system assume that the child prefers responsibility to dependency? As children mature, this assumption becomes increasingly sound and important. The current grading system makes the child dependent on his teacher and parents to do the evaluating for him. It rarely involves him in the evaluating process—except to ask him the lowest level questions, such as: Do you like it? What would you prefer? Why did you fail? Why did the teacher give you a C?

The child wants to become an independent person. He wants freedom to express his own ideas, select his own friends, experiment and try things out for himself. As part of the process of becoming a person who can bring about changes in himself, he needs to evaluate for himself some of the things he is doing and experiencing. He should have the freedom to make mistakes and the responsibility to learn from them.

We may agree with all this—theoretically. Yet some

outside force is always evaluating for the child without giving him a chance to evaluate for himself. It's all for his own good, we tell ourselves. So we criticize his friends and ridicule his way of speaking or dressing. We pressure him on homework and regulate his leisure hours. We censor his reading, select his toys, and arrange his summers. We choose his vocation for him.

The power of the report card

The child winds up evaluating the evaluators—his parents, his teachers, his school—rarely himself. He feels caught in a system. His report card becomes the source of privileges bestowed or taken away. It becomes the primary source of feeling successful or unsuccessful. It has the power to make parents and students proud or ashamed with great regularity. The report card has great manipulating power, the power to make a child a puppet.

Furthermore, the reporting system is so designed that it is constantly comparing a child to a group—his classmates or children of his grade level across the country. It rarely deals with individuality, with the individual as an individual. Perhaps that is why it is so easily computerized. Once we lock the system in the computer, it will be more difficult than ever to change. And change it we must.

Are we assuming that children want to achieve and to become real individuals—persons in their own right? This assumption would result in a more adequate system of evaluation than we now have, but it requires a great many subtle influences working in the home and the school at the same time. Parents and teachers would *expect* good workmanship. They would take it for granted that a child *wants* to do a good job. Parents would refrain from comparing a child with his brothers and sisters. They would value each child for himself; they would be aware and appreciate that he is uniquely different from all others in the family or in his class.

This respect for differences would affect children's attitudes toward the adults they need to respect and admire—the parents and teachers who influence their values. Children would see that adults can have different qualities that are admirable. Instead of comparing this year's teacher with last year's teacher merely in terms of the kind of "marker" he is, they might begin to see and respect the uniquely different qualities of various teachers.

Finally, are we asking "effectiveness" questions— questions that reveal whether or not or how much the reporting system contributes to the purposes of education and evaluation? The inadequacy of the present system is shown by the fact that we respond to it with quantity questions rather than quality ones. The schools want to know how many A, B, C, D, and E grades are given. The parents want to know who else got all A's. The students ask each other, "How many did you get?" (Depending on the climate of the schools, they could be asking about stars or about failures.)

Evaluating the evaluation system

The evaluation system we need to design must make all involved respond by asking effectiveness questions like these: Does the evaluation system deliver the feedback, the information, that is needed? Does it deliver the information when it is needed? And to the persons who need it?

To meet the test of effectiveness the system must satisfy the following criteria, set forth by the Association for Supervision and Curriculum Development in its 1967 yearbook, *Evaluation as Feedback and Guide:*

1. Evaluation must facilitate self-evaluation.

2. Evaluation must encompass every objective valued by the school.

3. Evaluation must facilitate learning and teaching.

4. Evaluation must provide continuing feedback into the larger questions of curriculum development and educational policy.

5. Evaluation must produce appropriate records.

When we consider these criteria it becomes apparent that problems of measurement and evaluation in

116

education are complex. The nature of the complexity makes the creation of any "new" system a highly professional task—a task that goes far beyond the poetic question "to grade or not to grade." It is a task that takes us into territory which is for the most part unmapped.

Work in progress

To meet the five criteria, educators and test-makers are trying to devise reliable, nonthreatening, helpful ways of measuring reading skills, writing ability and its components, ability in participating in small-group discussions and in carrying on independent study and experiments, and laboratory skills—to mention a few of the school's valued objectives. In addition we are trying to study what we call evaluative competence—that is, the evaluative skills, attitudes, and criteria of students. Here we are dealing with self-evaluation: the ability of a student to size up his own performance, growth, and potential.

In still other studies we are looking at individuality and the uniqueness of the person. We are trying to find out how individuals differ in their learning styles. We are asking, How do boys' styles of learning differ from girls'? How does each child express what he values? How does this information help us to understand him and build a curriculum for him? In these areas data are scarce. The questions are new questions (effectiveness ones), which, I believe, are extremely relevant for developing the kind of evaluation system we need.

In a new and better system, marks and grades as we now use them would become increasingly obsolete, for they never really help a student to view himself as a real person in the process of becoming. Proof of their inadequacy is the fact that all students—even the best or A students—worry about grades. Worry over marks is as universal among teenagers as their concern with self and sex. Marks certainly create more tension, perhaps because they become a part of the permanent school record. Imagine facing the constant prospect of being graded or evaluated every six weeks for the record. I doubt that many of us would tolerate

117

it in our jobs. We would probably become dropouts. Let's give the kids a break and overthrow the system before they do.

But a word of caution: Bear in mind that it is worse to have no system at all than one that is obsolete or one that we have outgrown. What then can parents do? Their best course is this: Help support what is good in the present system until a more adequate one is developed to replace it. Understand that evaluation is a highly professional task. Realize that the teaching staff will need the help of consultants and at least five years to explore and try out new methods of organizing, evaluating, and reporting. Be patient. And, finally, refuse to debate whether to grade or not to grade, for that is *not* the question.

Woodrow Mousley

REPORT CARDS ACROSS THE NATION

Few issues have occasioned more discussion among parents, teachers, and administrators than that of report cards.[1] In spite of prolonged effort on the part of schools to devise a better report card, a recent survey shows that over the years there has been very little improvement in the quality of such reports.

Reporting to Parents

One of the earliest records of a report card to parents appeared in Horace Mann's *Common School Journal* in 1840. The purpose of this early report was to solicit support from parents in improving the behavior and achievement of pupils. The writer of the article suggested sending different colored cards home to parents – a white card for "Entire Approbation," a blue card for "Approbation," a yellow card for "Indifferent," and a red card for "Censure."[2]

Early nineteenth-century report cards were often decorated with colored pictures of birds, butterflies, flowers, or other ornamentation. They usually carried the heading "Reward" or "Merit," the name of the student, and the name of the teacher. If a child excelled in reading, the card might be marked "For Superior Reading" or "To a Studious Child."

This era of decorative report cards which said very little was followed by the McGuffey Reader era in which the report card became more definitive, but only in the subject of reading. Report cards indicated the reading level by citing the graded book and the page completed by the student at the close of the school year. This was an attempt to tell more but, in fact, again told a parent very little.

The use of percents on report cards to indicate the student's academic growth was the next step. By the onset of the Civil War most elementary schools were graded and teacher-made tests were being used for determining the student's grade-level achievement. Percents on tests were used to indicate the degree of student success. These percentage grades were then used on report cards to show parents how their children stood. One hundred percent was established as perfect, with descending percents indicating less than perfect achievement.

Because of the difficulty of calculating scores to the nearest percent, this method soon gave way to the simpler and more inclusive A,B,C,D, and F designations. Percentage scores were not dropped but were translated into simple letter equivalents. The letter "A" represented 95-100%, "B" represented 85-94%, and so on. By 1900 the prac-

PHI DELTA KAPPAN, March 1972, pp. 426-427.

tice of assigning letter grades was established and by 1940 four-fifths of the elementary schools in the country had discontinued the use of percentages for reporting and were using some kind of letter grade designation.[3]

The 1930s saw the introduction of another step in the direction of oversimplification.[4] The pass-fail marks of "S" for satisfactory and "U" for unsatisfactory were used because of their utter simplicity. It was decided that if using five letters was good, the use of two letters would be even better. Many schools experimented with the pass-fail designation during the thirties and forties, only to give it up because it told parents so little.

Current National Trends

I recently surveyed a nationwide sample to determine the kinds of report cards currently used in elementary schools for reporting academic achievement. Two hundred school districts representing all 50 states were asked to send specimen copies of the report cards used in their districts. Districts from two large cities and two small towns were randomly selected from each state for inclusion in the survey. The first 100 returns are cited here and have been tallied in Table 1.

Academic achievement was reported in 10 different ways in the 100 report cards analyzed, while social adjustment was reported with the usual "Satisfactory," "Unsatisfactory," or "Needs Improvement."

Letter Grades. The survey showed that the letter grade method is by far the most popular way of reporting progress in both the primary and the upper elementary grades. Fifty-seven percent of the districts reported using letter grades in grades 1-3, 73% in grades 4-6. Some districts using letter grade designations varied the usual A,B,C,D,F with such letter combinations as A,B,C,D,E; E,S,I,N,U; E,G,S,U; A,B,C, D,E,F; A,B,C,D; A,B,C,D,U; or H,O,S,

L,I,U. The change in the letters represents an attempt on the part of some school districts to get away from the stereotype but at the same time retain the advantage of a simple rating scale. For example, in the combination H,O, S,L,I,U, which is presently used in the Cabell County, West Virginia, School District, the different letters stand for key words: "H" for "Honor Grade," "O" for "Outstanding Work," "S" for "Satisfactory," and so on.

Irrespective of the varying letter combinations, this method of reporting is a simple rating scale. In several instances percents are used in combination with letter grades, but the percent designation is never used alone. When in combination, A = 95-100%, B = 85-94%, C = 75-84%, D = 65-74%. Equivalent percents are given in the report card legend.

Check Lists. A check list for evaluating achievement was reported for only 13% of the report cards used in grades 1-3 and for only 2% of those used in grades 4-6. But check lists for evaluating personal attributes or social adjustment are widely used at all grade levels. Almost all report cards studied used some such list. Desired behavior traits or social adjustment were, in most cases, listed in a column, each item to be checked by the teacher as "Satisfactory," "Needs Improvement," etc.

Pass-Fail. The pass-fail method of reporting was used on only 6% of the report cards evaluated. Usage has declined since the 1930s, when it was experimented with so freely.

The terms "Satisfactory" and "Needs Improvement" have to some extent taken the place of pass-fail, or "Satisfactory" and "Unsatisfactory," at least in the primary grades. The terms "Satisfactory" and "Needs Improvement" were used 6% of the time in grades 1-3 and only 2% of the time in grades 4-6.

The low incidence of the use of pass-fail for indicating academic achievement, whether the designation is S-U or "Satisfactory" and "Needs Improvement," seems to indicate that most administrators believe that simplicity alone is not the answer to good reporting.

Percentage Grades. Percentage grades, popular at the turn of the century, were never used alone on any of the 100 report cards analyzed, only in conjunction with letter grades to give the letter grades a value.

The Need To Answer Questions

While there has been a continuous effort on the part of schools to find a better report card, the trend has by no means been one of continual improvement. For example, the use of the "S" and "U" for pass-fail could hardly be said to be an improvement, and yet report cards went from the use of percents to the A,B,C,D,F designation at the turn of the century, to pass-fail in the 1930s, and again to letter grades in the 1940s. Thus innovation abounds in many areas of the educational scene, but there is little that is new in report cards. The most popular kind of report 40 years ago is the most popular report today.

Our present report cards leave the following questions unanswered for parents:

1. Where does the child stand in relation to national norms?

2. Where does he stand in relation to his own ability?

3. What required skills did the child master during the school year?

4. What important concepts did the child acquire?

5. What skills and concepts should be programmed for each child in the following year?

6. What kind of ongoing evaluation can be used that will clearly indicate the dynamics of change, mastery, or achievement?

Surely in this age of computers, when man can literally fly to the moon, a better report form can be found — a report that answers some if not all of the above questions, that not only gives the student a printout of his progress and needs but also gives parents needed insight into the teaching-learning process and how it is affecting their child.

Table 1

A Comparison of Ten Different Ways
Academic Achievement Is Shown
on Report Cards and the Percentage
of Districts Using Them

Principal Ways of Reporting	Primary Grades (1-3) Percent Using Method	Upper Grades (4-6) Percent Using Method
Letter grade	57%	73%
Check list	13%	2%
Letter grade with percent equivalent	3%	11%
S = satisfactory I = improvement shown N = needs improvement	8%	2%
O = outstanding S = satisfactory N = needs improvement	6%	2%
S = satisfactory N = needs improvement	6%	2%
Pass-fail	4%	2%
Number grades such as 1,2,3,4,5 instead of letter grades	1%	4%
Letter grade plus national norm percentile equivalent	2%	2%
Percent only	0%	0%

This table is based on a nationwide survey of 100 elementary school districts, grades 1-6, summer, 1971.

1. Wilson F. Wetzler, "Reporting Pupil Progress," *Grade Teacher*, April, 1959, pp. 14-16.

2. Henry J. Otto, *Elementary School Organizations and Administration.* New York: Appleton-Century-Crofts, 1954.

3. William L. Wrinkle, *Improving Marking and Reporting Practices.* New York: Holt, Rinehart, 1947.

4. *Ibid.*

IS TESTING A MENACE TO EDUCATION?

Henry S. Dyer

THE TITLE of this talk is a question: "Is Testing a Menace to Education?" Knowing who I am and what I do for a living,* you would have every reason to believe that I am going to answer the question with a resounding, "No!" But you would be dead wrong, for I am going to answer the question with a tentative, "Yes, but—" Yes, testing *is* a menace to education, *but* probably not for the reasons you think. It is a menace to education primarily because tests are misunderstood and test results are misused by too many educators. In his recent book called *The Schools*, Martin Mayer speaks of testing as a "necessary evil." I disagree. It is not *necessarily* evil. Tests *could* be a blessing to education if only teachers and counselors and educational administrators would divest themselves of a number of misconceptions about what tests can and cannot do and would learn to use test results more cautiously and creatively in the educational process.

There are nine principal misconceptions that seem to stand in the way of the appropriate use of tests.

THE *FIRST* MISCONCEPTION is the notion that aptitude or intelligence tests measure something called "native ability," something fixed and immutable within the person that determines his level of expectation for all time. I am not prepared to say such an inherent entity does not exist. The chances are it does. Studies in genetics certainly support the idea, and so do many psychological studies. But intelligence or aptitude tests do not *measure* such an entity—at least not directly, and certainly not in any interpretable manner.

---

* Dr. HENRY S. DYER *is vice president for College Board Programs, Educational Testing Service, Princeton, N. J. This article is a condensation of an address Dr. Dyer gave before the presidents and secretaries of state education secretaries at the Traymore Hotel, Atlantic City, during the 1961 NEA Convention.*

NEW YORK STATE EDUCATION, October 1961, Vol. 49, pp. 16-19.

What intelligence tests do measure is the individual's performance on certain types of mental tasks . . . a long time after the child has first entered the world. The kinds of mental tasks that appear in any intelligence or aptitude test are clearly the kinds that a student *learns* to perform from his experiences in the world around him. The amount of learning based on such experiences may depend on many things that can vary enormously from one child to another—the number and quality of books available in his home, the kind of talk he hears, the richness and variety of his surroundings, the vividness and emotional quality of the thousands of happenings in his life from day to day. It is absurd to suppose that a child's score on an intelligence test by-passes all these factors, to suppose that such a score gets directly at the brains he was born with.

I prefer to think of an intelligence test as essentially indistinguishable from an achievement test—that is, as a measure of how well, at a given point of time, a student can perform certain well-defined tasks. The main difference between the tasks in a so-called achievement test and those in a so-called intelligence test is, generally speaking, that the tasks in an achievement test are usually learned over a relatively short time and those in an intelligence test are learned over a relatively long time.

THE CONSEQUENCES of thinking of an aptitude test as measuring some immutable determiner of student performance can be pretty serious. First, such thinking encourages the dangerous idea that one can, from an aptitude score, decide once and for all at a fairly early age what kind and level of educational or vocational activity a student is fitted for. It nurtures that hardy perennial, for instance, that if a student has an IQ of 115 or better he ought to prepare for college, and if his IQ is below 115 he ought to make other plans—this, despite all the studies which have shown that an IQ may be highly variable for a given student, that colleges vary enormously in the quality of students they enroll, and that some low scorers succeed in college while some high scorers fail. I have often wondered how many educational crimes are annually committed on the strength of the theory that intelligence tests measure something they cannot possibly measure.

123

A second consequence, almost as serious, is the conception that a student with a high aptitude score and low achievement scores (or low grades in school) is an "under-achiever"—another hardy perennial. It was exploded 30 years ago, but it is back and can lead to some rather distressing treatment of individual pupils. The diagnosis goes that a student with a high aptitude score and low achievement scores is "unmotivated" or "lazy" or suffering from some sort of emotional disturbance. Granted there may be some grounds for such diagnoses, nevertheless they are scarcely inferrable from the discrepancy in scores alone. And some new and possibly more useful insights about such students might be forthcoming if one frankly regarded the discrepancies simply as differences in performance on one kind of achievement test as compared to another.

Finally, the idea that aptitude tests are supposed to measure native ability leads to the persistent and embarrassing demand that they should be "culture free"; that if they are, as they must be, affected by the student's background of experience in school and at home, then *ipso facto*, they are "unfair" to the underprivileged. I wish we could get it *out* of people's heads that tests are unfair to the underprivileged and get it *into* their heads that it is the hard facts of social circumstance and inadequate education that is unfair to them. If educational opportunities are unequal, the test results will also be unequal.

A *SECOND* MISCONCEPTION about tests is the notion that a prediction made from a test score, or from a series of test scores, or from test scores plus other quantifiable data, are, or should be, perfectly accurate, and that if they are not, the tests must be regarded as no good. This fallacy arises from a confused conception of what constitutes prediction. There are some people—maybe most people—who think of prediction as simply an all-or-none, right-or-wrong business. If a test score predicts that Johnny will get B in American history, the score is right if he actually gets a B; it is wrong if he gets a B — or a C. I suppose this is a legitimate way of thinking about prediction in certain circumstances, but it is scarcely fair to the test and it may well be unfair to Johnny. A more meaningful and useful way of thinking about a prediction is to regard it as a statement of the odds: A given test score might predict that Johnny has 8 chances in 10 of getting a grade of B or better in American history, and 3 chances in a hundred of flunking. This approach recognizes that in forecasting future events, especially human events, we never have sufficient information to be sure of being right every time, but we do have information, in the form of test scores and other data, which, if appropriately organized, can help us make better decisions than would be possible without them.

THE *THIRD* MISCONCEPTION is that standardized test scores are infallible or perfectly reliable. Reliability, I remind you, has to do with the degree to which the score of an individual stands still on successive testings. It rarely occurs to the uninitiated that a test can never be more than a *sample* of a student's performance and that, in consequence, the score on any test is afflicted with sampling error. To the man-in-the-street, to many teachers, school administrators and parents, who have never reflected on the problem, a score is a score is a score, and they are shocked to find that when a student takes one test today and an alternate form of the same test tomorrow, his score can change. Anyone who deals with a test score must always be conscious that such a score, like any sort of measurement whatever, is clouded with uncertainty, that it is never more than an estimate of the truth.

A *FOURTH* MISCONCEPTION is the assumption that an achievement test measures all there is to measure in any given subject matter area—that an achievement test in history, for example, measures everything a high school student should know about the facts of history and how to deal with them. It never seems to occur to some people that the content of a standardized achievement test in any particular subject matter area may be only partially related to what a specific course of study in that area may call for.

If people will only take the trouble to look critically at the insides of achievement tests and not just at their covers, they will almost certainly find that even the test best suited to their purposes still fails to sample *all* the types of learning that are sought in a given subject, or even all the most important types of learning. And it may also often include matters that the student is not expected to know. The consequence is, of course, that on a particular standardized achievement test a student may look considerably better or considerably worse than he really is, and decisions based on his score may miss the boat by a considerable margin.

A *FIFTH* MISCONCEPTION is that an achievement test can measure only a pupil's memory for facts. This used to be true. But a good modern achievement test gets at far more than a command of facts alone; it usually measures in addition the pupil's skill in reasoning with the facts he remembers and also his skill in reasoning with facts newly presented to him. It is this introduction into achievement tests of the requirement to reason, to cope with problems, to think clearly, critically and even creatively that helps to blur the distinction between aptitude and achievement tests. The modern achievement test recognizes that as students come up through the grades they are, or ought to be, learning to think as well as to know. It recognizes also that there may be many different kinds of thinking to measure, depending upon the subject matter in which the thinking is required. The result is that a well-conceived battery of achievement tests gives the same sort of information one would get from a general intelligence test plus a good deal more.

A *SIXTH* MISCONCEPTION has to do with profiles of achievement or aptitude scores, that a profile of scores summarizes clearly and efficiently a considerable amount of reliable information about the relative strengths and weaknesses of an individual. Test technicians have inveighed repeatedly against the use of profile charts on the grounds that they are often grossly misleading, that the differences they depict—even when they appear large—may be, and usually are, unreliable differences, that the score scales used for the several tests in the profile may not be comparable, that the several measures which show on the profile may have the appearance of being highly independent measures when, in fact, many of them may be highly correlated—in short, that the apparent clarity and efficiency of a test score profile is really an illusion covering up all sorts of traps and pitfalls in score interpretation which even the most wary can scarcely avoid.

Yet the profile chart is still in much demand and in wide use, primarily, I suppose, because it is extraordinarily convenient. Mere administrative convenience is hardly sufficient justification for hiding confusion under a false coat of simplicity. Good test interpretation takes mental effort, a bit of imagination and some willingness to cope with complexity.

A *SEVENTH* MISCONCEPTION is that interest inventories measure some kind of basic orientation of a student irrespective of the kinds of experiences to which he has been or will be exposed. Let me cite just one example. A presumably well-trained guidance counselor in a high school where the large majority of students go on to college was confronted by a girl with top-notch scholastic standing in all of the college preparatory subjects. Her parents were college trained people, had always expected their daughter would go to a liberal arts college; the daughter had always enthusiastically entertained the same idea. The counselor, however, was apparently bewitched by one of the girl's scores on an interest inventory which indicated her major interest was in clerical work. Disregarding all the other evidence, the counselor insisted that the girl was unfitted for the work of a liberal arts college and would be happy only in a secretarial school. Tears on the part of the child, anger on the part of the parents and hell-to-pay all around. Certainly interest test scores are useful in promoting thought and self-analysis, but certainly also the tests are scarcely capable of probing deeply enough into an individual's past and future to warrant anything approaching the dogmatism which characterized this counselor.

THE *EIGHTH* MISCONCEPTION is that on a personality test an individual reveals deep and permanent temperamental characteristics of which he himself may be unaware. I suppose there is nothing about the whole testing business that frightens me more than this. Anyone close to the research in personality testing who has any critical sense at all knows that we have still barely scratched the surface of a field whose dimensions are still far from defined. To put it perhaps a little too strongly, personality tests—the inventories, the projective tests, all of them—are scarcely beyond the tea-leaf-reading stage. To be sure, there is some interesting—even exciting—research going on in the area, but none of it yet adds up to tests that can be trusted as evidence leading to important decisions about children.

There are four major weaknesses in personality tests. First, they purport to measure traits such as introversion-extraversion, neurotic tendency, gregariousness, tolerance for ambiguity, and the like—all of which are highly fuzzy concepts, to say the least, and for none of which there are any agreed upon definitions. There is not even any general agreement on what we mean by the word "personality" itself. How can you describe or classify a person meaningfully with a test whose scores do not themselves have any clear or rigorous meaning?

Secondly, it is characteristic of current personality tests that the behavior they sample is essentially superficial nonsignificant behavior. By this I mean when a subject answers such a question as "Do you often daydream?" his response of "Yes" or "No" may well be nothing more than a purely random phenomenon quite unconnected with any of his habitual behavior tendencies. The whole essence of the measurement problem is to secure reliable samples of human behavior under standardized conditions which will have strong correlates with the universe of behavior an individual habitually exhibits in his waking life. The personality tests currently available have yet to demonstrate that they can provide such samples.

Thirdly, even if we were able to establish some meaningful personality traits, we still know little or nothing about their stability. We still don't know whether an introvert at age 15 may not turn into an extravert by the time he is 22.

Finally, of course, practically all personality tests can be fakes. I proved to my own satisfaction how fakable such tests are when I gave one to a class I was once teaching. I asked the students to take a personality inventory twice—once to prove that they were thoroughly well-adjusted people and once to prove that they were ready for a mental institution. The first set of scores showed that the whole class was a bunch of apple-cheeked extraverts; the second set showed that they were all nuts.

Please do not misunderstand me. I take a very dim

view of current personality tests, and I think the general public is being much too frequently taken in by the mumbo-jumbo that goes with them. On the other hand, I am very much in favor of as much solid research as we can possibly get into the fundamental dynamics of human behavior, for we shall never be in full command of the educational process until we have far more understanding than we now have of what makes children tick. There are glimmerings of hope, but we are not out of the woods yet, and who can tell when we will be? In the meantime, let's not kid ourselves by putting our trust in gimmicks.

THE *NINTH* AND FINAL MISCONCEPTION is this: that a battery of tests can tell all one needs to know in making a judgment about a student's competence, present and potential, and about his effectiveness as a human being. The fact is that no test or series of tests now available is capable of giving the total picture of any child. Tests can illuminate many areas of his development, suggest something about his strengths and weaknesses, show in certain respects how he stands among his peers. But there are still many important aspects of learning and human development where we must still rely upon the observation and judgment of teachers if we are to get something that approaches a complete description of the child as a functioning individual. There are subtle but supremely important human elements in the teaching-learning situation that no combination of tests yet devised is able to capture. Such elements are elusive, but if ever we lose sight of them, the educational process in all its ramifications will become something less than the exciting human enterprise it should always be.

THESE ARE the nine misconceptions which I think most frequently lead to wide misuse of tests and test results. Some of our brasher critics have argued that, since tests are so widely misused, they do constitute a menace to sound education and therefore should be abolished. This argument is specious. It is the same as saying that automobiles should be abolished because they are a menace to human life when reckless drivers are at the wheel. Or it is the same as saying that teachers should be abolished because too many of them make psychometric hash out of marks and test scores.

In any case, I think it is highly unlikely that tests will be abolished anymore than that textbooks will be abolished. Too many schools have discovered that, menace or not, they cannot operate effectively without them. The problem is not one of doing away with tests and testing but of getting people to use tests intelligently. When this happens testing will cease to be a mere administrative convenience or, worse still, a burden on the souls of teachers and pupils; it will become an effective instrument for vitalizing the total educational process and for helping to insure that in these days of skyrocketing enrollments the individual pupil will not be lost in the shuffle.

DISCIPLINE IS . . .

Sister Helena Brand, SNJM

Formulas for maintaining classroom discipline are many and varied, and what works for one teacher fails for another. Chances are, nonetheless, that any formula that proves effective is more preventive than remedial and contains the following ingredients:

Discipline is preparation—long-range and short-range. Long-range preparation is the necessary daily routine of planning, preparing material, and correcting papers.

Short-range preparation is the activity just before a class begins that results in students' entering an orderly room. The teacher has all the necessary materials ready for distribution. He has written key words on the board to guide students in following his instructions and to make oral spelling unnecessary. He adjusts windows, arranges his books, checks his seat plan, and prepares his attendance slip. The classroom is ready, and the teacher is in control. Class begins promptly without that little lull in which attention is often lost before it is even captured.

Discipline is dignity. In the classroom, the teacher lives his dignity by avoiding casual sitting positions, casual vocabulary, casual joking, familiar give-and-take—except when they are deliberately used as tools of emphasis.

Dignity expects the courtesy of a greeting when pupils come into the classroom. The teacher will not receive acknowledgment from every student, but his attitude will encourage many greetings.

Since the teacher expects the class to consider education a serious business, he approaches his class in a businesslike, professional way. He is courteous, considerate, pleasant, understanding, consistent, and, in the sum, dignified.

TODAY'S EDUCATION—NEA JOURNAL, September 1965, pp. 26-28.

Discipline is moving deliberately and purposefully with the apparent self-confidence of a captain on top-deck. The disciplined teacher shows that he knows exactly what he wants to do. By acting serene, he creates an atmosphere of serenity. Students assume the matter-of-fact, reasonable, practical tones and attitudes of their teachers. Generally, a student is as tense or relaxed as his teacher.

Discipline is speaking distinctly with a pleasant, friendly voice. Students will listen more attentively and ask questions more spontaneously if the "sound effects" are pleasant and harmonious. Tape recording a few periods and playing them back can reveal to the teacher poor speech habits, such as lack of tone variation or overly numerous "uh's," that detract from presentations.

The teacher who does not speak simply or slowly enough for his students to understand easily may find that students release their feeling of frustration and inadequacy by finding compensating entertainment. When a student stops doing what the teacher wants him to do, he begins to do what he is tempted to do.

Discipline is teaching a subject in terms of the interest level of the class. The vocabulary challenges at times, but it is within the understanding of the class. Good current allusions, based on newspaper or magazine articles, are attention-getters which act as springboards to new lessons.

Discipline is questions and answers from the students. A discussion sparked by a student's questions is usually lively because interest is tapped and channeled. The best answer is the student answer. The teacher whose students not only raise questions but reason their way to the right answers practices a special kind of personal discipline. He controls his very human tendency to save time by "just telling" the class the answers. The right answer formulated by the students does more for their development than the most dynamically articulated answer the teacher could produce.

Discipline is utilizing the natural tendencies of the students. Carefully planned group discussions and buzz sessions, or occasions when students plan and take responsibility for their own activity, give

132

the students the chance to express their desires and clarify their purposes. They also allow the young people to experience the success of influencing their group and to grow in personal security. Such sessions give students a legitimate reason for speaking as opposed to reciting during a class period, and for moving to another part of the room.

Discipline is perceiving and understanding causes of misbehavior. The perceptive teacher notices the student who comes to class burning with resentment and rebellion. Aware that he may have had trouble at home that morning or in his previous class, the teacher avoids any conflict which will aggravate the student's sense of injury and result in sullenness, insolence, or even violence.

The teacher realizes that many, if not all, of his students suffer from feelings of inferiority or inadequacy. Particularly affected are those who may feel out of the "in-group" because they are of a different race or religion, because they lack money, or because they cannot keep up mentally or physically.

The wise teacher knows that publicly demeaning a student or in any way implying rejection or ridicule is inviting misbehavior, which is often a defense mechanism.

Discipline is realizing that students are human beings. Students leave books and pencils at home (teachers forget things, too). To punish a student's forgetfulness by keeping him idle is retaliatory rather than remedial. The youngster feels conspicuous, frustrated; above all, he feels a sense of injury. The better course is for the teacher to provide the missing article and thus have a busy rather than a humiliated student. The "little talk" for chronic amnesia victims can come at the end of the period when he returns the article the teacher has loaned him.

Being human, students appreciate recognition. They are happy to be in charge of something. They are proud to be sent on errands, glad to be noticed in the hall.

When papers are returned, a comment by the teacher praising a mark, remarking on the completeness of a particular answer, or noting the neat attractive format or script, not only excites ambition but also promotes a pleasant teacher-pupil relationship. The morning after a play, a recital, or a game, the student who is complimented on his outstanding participation is an appreciative, cooperative person.

Discipline is knowing when to tighten, when to loosen, and when to hold firm. A class changes its mood with the weather, with the exciting rally students screamed through during the noon hour, with the warm library period they have just sat out, with the way things went in the last class, with the pictures that appeared in the morning's issue of the school paper. Students come into the classroom with an attitude toward the teacher engendered, perhaps, by their success or nonsuccess with the assignment.

Sometimes students come in quietly, sometimes in a stampede, sometimes laughing, sometimes bitterly arguing. The bell momentarily cuts off their stream of interest, and into this small space the teacher drives the line of action he expects the class to follow through the period. He directs their vitality. By clear, simply spoken instructions he puts them to work.

If directions offer personal advantages to the students as individuals, the class as a whole will settle down. An effective means to calm a class is to have written recitation during the first ten or fifteen minutes. The teacher remarks that the lesson is of more than usual importance. He wants to credit every individual who has done the assignment with a successful recitation. Since it takes too long for each student to recite, each may earn a recitation credit by choosing two of the four questions to write on. Even if they do not finish writing in the allotted time, the work they have completed will indicate the quality of their preparation and the papers will be scored with that in mind.

Another time, he may have the student decide on the question or topic he found most interesting and then write on it for ten minutes. Students set to work with an optimistic spirit, glad to put their best answers forward. Just before they begin writing, the teacher directs their attention to the next day's assignment on the chalkboard. He suggests that if they finish the class exercise before the time is up, they look over the new material. He will answer any questions on the new assignment after the writing session is terminated. He indicates that the rest of the class period will be a build-up for the assigned work. Looking to their personal advantage, the students generally cooperate.

Sometimes a class needs waking up instead of calming down. On Monday, perhaps, when students are recuperating from a busy weekend (or giving the impression that they had the kind of weekend that requires recuperation), a buzz session can be profitable. It gives students an opportunity to compare notes, improve their homework papers, argue, and wake up.

Discipline is anticipating difficulties. The misbehaving individual makes a problem for the teacher, and also for the class. During the first month of school the teacher checks without exception infringements of class or school regulations. One individual who "gets away with it" breeds others who will try. Planning for emergencies and anticipating problems develops and maintains teacher control, strengthens students' confidence in the teacher's authority. and establishes a receptive classroom atmosphere.

Finally, discipline is having effective attitudes. Effective attitudes stimulate pupils to action. Creative thinking develops in the classroom of a teacher who shows that he appreciates a student's point of view. An instructor who is really thrilled with his subject effectively presents it as an intellectual adventure, a colorful discovery that induces similar excitement in his students. An instructor who shows interest in student affairs, who not only listens to student problems but contributes to their solutions, is an effective teacher in the classroom, in the conference room, in the give-and-take of a lunch-room situation.

TEACHERS' discipline is essentially self-discipline. The young teacher who is hopeful yet fearful, ambitious yet humble, idealistic yet practical, with everything to give, with everything to lose, will find his success in proportion to his ability to know himself and to use that knowledge in personal and professional growth.

135

THE USE OF BEHAVIOR MODIFICATION BY STUDENT TEACHERS—A CASE STUDY IN CONTINGENCY MANAGEMENT

William Ray Heitzmann

During the spring semester of 1971 I introduced the concept of contingency contracting* to a student teacher following my observation of a class which contained a disruptive student.

The student teacher, unknown to the student, counted the number of "unauthorized talkouts" for three consecutive days. These "talkouts" numbered thirteen (13), fourteen (14), and thirteen (13). At this point the student was approached by the student teacher and asked if he would like to sign a contract in which he would agree to limit his "unauthorized talkouts" to an average of two (2) per day or a total of six (6) for three days. The reward to be given by the student teacher was a picture of Howard Porter, Villanova basketball star. Teacher and student both signed the contract.

Unfortunately the student was unable to meet his requirements of the contract—"unauthorized talkouts" numbered seven (7), six (6), and zero (0). This was complicated by two weeks of team teaching and two "snow days" when he was not in his regular classroom.

The student teacher and I decided that because of the improvement shown, the student deserved another chance, with an improved reward—the picture of Howard Porter with a note written to the student signed by Porter. A new contract was signed by both parties.

The student completed his requirements for the contract—"unauthorized talkouts"—two (2), three (3), one (1). He received the reward.

This was a learning experience for all involved; in fact, the above experiment was presented to the student teaching seminar for discussion. Follow-up (post reward) data were collected—"unauthorized talkouts"—two (2), one (1), two (2). This behavior was the best of any period observed. In addition the student showed significant academic improvement.

* Contingency contracting is a form of behavior modification in which a contract is signed. It attempts to reward one party for performing a desired behavior or omitting undesirable behavior.

THE TEACHER EDUCATOR, Winter 1971-72, vol. 7, p. 36.

Bryan L. Lindsey and James W. Cunningham

BEHAVIOR MODIFICATION: SOME DOUBTS AND DANGERS

For some time "the modification of behavior" has been the textbook definition of learning, but "behavior modification" has been redefined to focus more on discipline than on intellectual growth. It seeks to mold human behavior by arranging the events in a learner's environment so that he responds in a desirable and predictable direction. These contingencies are managed by offering rewards for acceptable behavior and by withholding rewards for unacceptable behavior.

There are a number of inconsistencies in logic and some serious dangers involved in the use of behavior modification techniques in group and classroom situations. If behavior modification is used:

1. *It makes discipline a system of rewards,* which is no better than making it a system of punishments; good discipline is more than rewards and punishment; it is progress toward mutually established and worthwhile goals. A good disciplinarian is a leader who instigates and directs action toward these goals without great dependence on rewards or punishments but with an awareness of what to teach and how to teach it.

2. *It prepares students for a nonexistent world;* to ignore unacceptable behavior is to socialize for an unexisting society. An important aspect of most

behavior modification is to disregard, as much as possible, inappropriate behavior. Society and nature do not ignore such behavior.

3. *It undermines existing internal control.* Behavior modification is a system to modify behavior in a classroom. But if students showing internal control in a class are learning, why should they be externally rewarded? Might they not then stop being self-directed and begin working only for external rewards?

4. *It is unfair.* To refrain from externally rewarding the behavior of some students for fear of weakening their internal control is to be faced with the alternative of providing rewards only for those without internal control. It will seem unfair to the students who have been doing what is expected of them without reward, while those having difficulty in doing what is expected of them are being rewarded. A point system or other reinforcement schedule shows a major weakness if allowance is made for individual differences, in that students already behaving in acceptable ways will remain unrewarded, while those exhibiting unacceptable behavior will be rewarded ("paid off") on occasions when they show modified behavior. But if no allowance is made for individual differences, students having a history of unacceptable behavior will

PHI DELTA KAPPAN, May 1973, pp. 596-597.

137

receive fewer total rewards than those who can easily conform and obtain maximum rewards.

5. *It could instruct children to be mercenary.* A system of rewards or punishments or both requires the teacher to decide how much conformity or nonconformity is enough. Since the student is exposed to many teachers with divergent standards of behavior, he could easily become confused about what acceptable behavior is and conclude that it is whatever is profitable in a material sense.

6. *It limits the expression of student discontent.* Unacceptable classroom behavior is often an indication that content and methods used in teaching are inappropriate for the needs of students. To this extent, such behavior is healthy; it is evidence that change is in order. A system of rewards or punishments which causes students to accept instruction they should reject might make it seem less necessary to modify that instruction, and thus limit student input into the curriculum.

7. *It denies human reasoning.* Many parents and teachers treat with ridicule the practice of reasoning with children about their behavior and academic performance. But despite the obvious imperfections of man, history and contemporary times are evidence of his overall good sense and practicality. A system of rewards which would "pay" for acceptable behavior and academic effort surrenders the appeal of the reasonableness of what the child is expected to do, substituting payoffs. The denial of reason, the opposite extreme from always reasoning with children, is no less ridiculous.

8. *It teaches action/reaction principles.* The complexity of human behavior is not adequately considered, since behavior modification uses action/reaction principles where there may be no logical action/reaction pattern for the learner, but only for the teacher (manipulator). Such techniques deal with behavior in the cognitive domain when behavior should be dealt with in all domains. For behavior to be internalized, it is best that it be understood by the individual whose behavior is being changed.

9. *It encourages students to "act" as if they are learning, in order to obtain rewards.* Once the range of acceptable behaviors is established by the teacher, the student will be able to affect responses within that range, causing the teacher to assume that desired behavior patterns are being established, when in fact the student is merely "playing the game."

10. *It emphasizes short-range rather than long-range effects.* It emphasizes to a fault the conditions under which learning is to take place rather than appropriately emphasizing what the outcome should be. This limitation results in fragmented educational experiences, and may result in long-term ill effects.

11. *It would make the student assume a passive role in his own education.* Behavior modification focuses the student's attention on behavioral responses that are acceptable by the teacher, thus limiting the choice of behaviors for the student. This could result in frustration of personal goals toward creativity and self-actualization, weakening individual motives.

12. *It is a totalitarian concept in which the behavior shown by an individual is regarded as more important than the state of affairs in the individual's life leading to his behavior.* The use of behavior modification techniques is very often an attack upon symptoms of problems rather than an attack upon problems. Because it makes teachers the sole legitimizers of classroom behavior, it gives them an "out" from really confronting the problems met in teaching children.

Discipline and the Disadvantaged Child

by Alfred P. Hampton

"Discipline, like education, must fit both the situation and the child," says Mr. Hampton in exploring discipline problems unique to the disadvantaged child.

Parents in disadvantaged homes usually have standards and values which are comparable to those of so-called middle-class families. But economics. lack of privacy and sheer necessity to survive make it virtually impossible for many adults in a severely deprived environment to give more than lip service to such standards.

Abandoning hope for themselves, they cling to the one remaining dream—that their children shall some day be able to live differently.

They say, in effect, "Don't do as I do; do as I say!"

NEW YORK STATE EDUCATION, April 1969, pp. 19-21, 50.

They thus impose a dual standard. The inconsistency is quickly sensed by the child, and he resents it. His parents, not realizing that education literally begins at home with the assimilation of adult behavior patterns, see nothing unreasonable in demanding that the child obey. When he rebels, as he does early on, they impose harsher, more unyielding strictures than the middle-class parent is ever likely to invoke.

The small child, of course, has no alternative but to comply. As an accommodation to his environment, he develops a superficial response, a respectful, obedient manner. But his frustration and anger, only temporarily suppressed, lie not far beneath, waiting a chance for release. This is not to say that center-city parents fail to love their children, or that center-city children do not love their parents. As we all know, a child may have conflicting reactions which encompass both love and resentment. As he grows older, the regimen of fiat and fear to which he is subjected at home—for his own good, from his parents' point of view—increases the suppressed resentment and leads in his teenage years to outright hostility, not only toward his parents but also toward every authority symbol he encounters.

If I took you along with me to visit homes in deprived areas of the city, you might be amazed at how well-behaved the youngsters seem, especially some children who are already beginning to develop problem behavior traits in the classroom. At home, their manners are excellent and they appear to respect their parents.

Comparing their conduct at home with their conduct in school, you might ask: What are we doing wrong in the classroom?

But it should be remembered that aggression is usually manifested first outside the home. For one thing, the young pre-adolescent is still dependent on his home, emotionally and for the necessities of life, such as they are. Moreover, he is vastly more afraid to displease his parent than to displease his teacher, for he has learned that retribution for bad conduct at home is swift and physically painful.

Away from home, the child is likely to become progressively more aggressive toward everyone. Policemen are referred to as "dirty cops," teachers as "old bags," and even his own friends as "fakes."

As his attitude deteriorates, we in the schools become alarmed. We roll up our sleeves, open up our psychology books and invite in the experts in an attempt to find some way to help the hard-to-handle youngster. We have, indeed, made advances in this area and we should continue to seek new techniques and arrangements through which we can better serve these boys and girls.

At the same time, we must view the job to be done as twofold. We must seek to increase our understanding of the center-city milieu and culture, specifically, our understanding of the center-city parent or other adult who stands *in loco parentis* to the disadvantaged child. We must learn to work with these adult figures as well as with the student himself.

Unless we can find some way to educate the parents, and thus to change the center-city home environment significantly, youngsters from disadvantaged areas will continue to bring resentment and conflict into the classroom.

First, let us examine some of the causes why parents or guardians in the center-city milieu are so authoritarian.

To begin with, housing, especially for the Negro, is always a problem. It is not unusual for eight persons to exist in a three-and-a-half room apartment. As many as four or five youngsters, boys and girls, may share one room. In a situation such as this, the belt, ironing cord or the back of the parent's hand is the quickest, most convenient tool for maintaining order. One has only to visit such a home to witness the mother's role as policeman. In her hand is strap or stick. The phonograph is playing, the television blaring, the baby crying.

Constant hubub and lack of privacy, common to the crowded center-city apartment, tend to immunize children and adults to noise. These children are able to tune on or tune off at will: they hear what they wish to hear. It is not surprising, therefore, that they seem inattentive or appear to be poor listeners when they enter school. Because many of them do not follow directions and have short attention spans as a result of constant noise and distraction at home, they are often erroneously classified as retarded or borderline children.

In some disadvantaged homes, we find parents who are embittered, who are distrustful of the white "establishment." Their goals for their children may be extremely high. If the child lacks the ability to reach these goals, the parents do not accept this fact; they believe he is being discriminated against by white teachers and principals. Their anger spills over onto the child, especially if he brings home a poor report card, for which offense he will generally receive a belting. Such parents also become alarmed and resentful when teachers question the behavior of their children. Again, it is not difficult to see why. At home, Johnny has learned in self defense to be cooperative, almost docile. At school, the lid blows off. He is belligerent, openly defiant of all authority. But the parent simply doesn't believe it.

Another characteristic of the disadvantaged milieu is the home with one parent, a woman. These women love and are deeply concerned about their children. Their own insecurity is often manifested, however, in preoccupation with detail—Did you wash your face? Comb your hair? Brush your teeth? Make your bed, etc.?

Theirs is a heartbreaking task, at best. They must be both mother and father to their offspring, and they must work long hours to provide the bare necessities of life. They have little time and less energy to expend in visiting the school, conferring with the principal or finding out anything about the child's progress. Yet they may be eager to receive a home-school counselor or other school person who will come to see them in their own homes and talk with them as peer rather than patron.

One word of warning, however. It would be a grave error to stereotype all center-city parents. Many parents who have little or no education and whose incomes are marginal still manage to do a very good job of rearing their children. What they lack in the way of middle-class amenities, they make up for in other wholesome family activities. With just a little encouragement, disadvantaged families like this can be drawn into the school orbit, can become active members of the PTA, can develop real pride in and respect for the school system.

We recognize of course that there are, among the disadvantaged as among any economic group, adults who are not interested in their children or who have such severe emotional problems that they are incapable of being good parents. These cases present special problems for the schools, whether the families be economically privileged or deprived.

Now let us consider some characteristics and needs of the disadvantaged child. In a democracy, it is the obligation of the school and of each teacher to accept each youngster, to take him where we find him and lead from that point.

If the disadvantaged child's language is poor, his vocabulary minimal; if he speaks in words and phrases rather than sentences, it is our job to help, not criticize or condemn.

But I cannot overemphasize one point: These children do not need teacher's overt pity or sympathy. In fact, they will be quick to take advantage of it. Like all youngsters, they're glad to find a loophole.

They need limitations, spelled out goals, and a feeling that their teachers believe in them as individuals. Specific instructions geared to the child's ability offer the disadvantaged child a framework of security which he badly needs. He wants to please, and should be able to achieve success by being given tasks which it is possible for him to accomplish, with a little effort.

Building rapport may be the teacher's first job in working with disadvantaged children, for they tend to keep their defenses up until they are sure they can trust you.

The whole question of corporal punishment is involved here. Even though some disadvantaged parents are sometimes strict and use physical force in punishing their children, they nonetheless deeply resent it when any other adult "lays hands" on the child. Especially if that adult is a white stranger, who may be suspect, per se, to the Negro parent.

Just as they admonish their youngsters to "behave" in school, so also do they warn them that they're not to "take anything" from anyone—meaning take no physical abuse from the white establishment.

The teacher's greatest weapon, therefore, is love, understanding and a good healthy dose of adult humility. We aren't God and just integrating a classroom isn't going to solve all our problems.

As educators, we must realize that just mixing children of different races, creeds and abilities isn't going to guarantee good education. We have also to experiment with new ideas, find ways to individualize the program for each child, use cross grouping, large-group small-group techniques, and any other method we can think of to meet the needs of the children involved. For we know that any child, regardless of his socio-economic background, becomes disruptive if he is insecure, if he is too far behind the class, or if he is so far ahead that he isn't challenged.

Some civil rights spokesmen have accused the schools of trying to impose middle-class standards. I see nothing wrong with trying to inculcate standards and values; in fact, this is one of the school's most important functions. Yet, it is true that we must pause now and then to evaluate those standards. Is it possible for every child to meet them? If not, how can they be revised without lowering our aspirations? Should every child be expected to conform to all rules? Or can some rules profitably be changed or stretched? How can we bring the disadvantaged child into the mainstream?

I certainly do not have all the answers. If I did, I could collect a magician's royalties. However, I do believe that the successful teacher is the pragmatic teacher, the teacher who adapts the ongoing program of education to the raw material, the children. Understanding each child and treating him as a worthwhile individual is the key, as we all know.

Too many rules can be just as foolish as none at all, and rules are made to be broken as well as to be followed. On the other hand, discipline should and must be consistent from day to day. Children want and need the security which derives from reasonable limitations.

Of course, we must always watch our own subconscious biases. This is nothing new. It has always been difficult not to like some children better than others, even in a classroom which is racially and socio-economically homogeneous. The problem is compounded, however, in the integrated classroom because disadvantaged children are acutely sensitive to the attitudes of adults in authority. They will not respond to the teacher who, for whatever reason, fails to treat all pupils with uniform fairness.

Example: Teacher emphasizes at the beginning of the year that she will have no arguments in her class. The children are told that any hitting or name calling is to be reported to the teacher, who will then solve the problem. This arrangement appears to be working very well for several weeks. Some incidents are reported and the teacher does a good job of classroom counseling. But one day a little boy reports that he has been called a racial name. The teacher reminds him that "sticks and stones will break your bones but words will never hurt you." She seems cross because he has reported this name-calling incident. Very shortly, he becomes one of that teacher's most difficult behavior cases.

This boy is convinced that the teacher has been hypocritical from the outset. He is disillusioned. Not only has he no further motivation to seek the teacher's approval, he is now actually motivated to be deliberately "bad," so as to get even.

Why did this teacher fail? Maybe she didn't feel well that particular day. Maybe she honestly thought the incident was too minor to be important. Perhaps she felt insecure about discussing anything which had racial overtones. Or perhaps she had some hidden prejudices. In any event, all of us must aim at the greatest degree of self-understanding if we are to understand our pupils. We may fool ourselves about our own biases, but it's virtually impossible to fool children.

Praise is another valuable tool in the positive-discipline kit. If a child does a job to the best of his ability, even though his work may be poor by more objective standards, reward him with praise. Tell him or write a note on his paper, or give him a gold star, or call his parents and tell them that he has worked very hard. One small success leads to a larger one, and that one leads to another even larger success.

This is not to say that teachers should be all sweetness and light. Legitimate anger has very definite value. Children expect it, in fact, when they know they are being disobedient or careless. If a teacher is justifiably angry, she should let the child know she isn't pleased. Her displeasure may be conveyed in her voice and attitude, or she may write a note on the child's paper indicating her disappointment. The important thing is not to carry over this anger so that it assumes the dimensions of a "grudge." Iron out differences that very day, before the child leaves for the day. And then start tomorrow with a clean page. Never let a child think you have lost confidence in him or that you view him as incorrigible.

Discipline has many facets other than punishment. Too often, we adults put children in a situation where they react negatively in order to save face. I have found, however, that even the toughest child will accept discipline if the approach is skillful and considerate. When a child is causing confusion in a group obstreperous student. But this same youngster is almost certain to be defiant, talk back and even use foul language if he is corrected in front of his peers. A child with a "repu-setting, such as classroom, hall or cafeteria, it's advisable to call him aside and lay the law down privately. Talking quietly with a disruptive pupil and showing him that you are disappointed in his behavior is usually a highly effective method and one which sometimes brings tears to the eyes of an ordinarily tation" to defend cannot back down in front of an audience.

I have said little about punishment, because I believe it is seldom necessary if discipline is regarded as an art and practiced accordingly. Punishment should be a last resort, after every other technique has been tried. And punishment should always fit the offense. Making a pupil write one thousand times "I will be good" is likely only to make him hate writing. A student could more beneficially be required to remain after school or stay indoors at recess to write a page on how and why he should be a good citizen. This is a logical punishment, which the child will recognize as such, and it is also sound educationally. The student is actually performing an English assignment as well as being put in a position where he must give some thought to his behavior and its implications.

Again, it does little good to correlate the length of an after-school penalty with the seriousness of a pupil's offense. A child can repent just as well in half an hour as in two hours, and he is more likely to do so. Time beyond the first half hour or so is quite likely to be spent in making plans for vengeance on the morrow. Certainly the staying-after-school procedure or any other punishment should be reinforced with an explanation of your point of view, the reasons for the regulations involved and for the punishment.

Discipline, like education, must fit both the situation and the child, and it is difficult to make many specific suggestions. Generally, I believe the guidelines which have worked best in my experience are these: Set limitations for your pupils and be firm when necessary. Be fair. Do not overemphasize small, unimportant things. Try to place youngsters in a position which will enable them to achieve some success. Be generous with your praise. Keep every child as busy as possible. Most important, try to love each child.

One final thought. Effective discipline is not only the key to a good educational experience for each pupil, it is also the key to a happy teaching experience.

146

SUBURBIA:

A Wasteland of Disadvantaged Youth and Negligent Schools?

By JAMES A. MEYER

The time has come to include our suburbias in any comprehensive assessment of the strengths and weaknesses of American education. At least among the vast middle classes, suburban life has long been thought of as ideal and suburban educational systems as exemplary; but there is mounting evidence that even by conventional standards such is not the case. One need look no further than the suburban youth—products of our so-called social utopias—to suspect that suburban societies and their educational institutions have been overrated and underproductive.

Indeed, suburban youth can no longer be taken for granted. How can they be, considering today's frightening world of aimless youth? The average suburban teen-ager is often pictured as either consumed with self pity or alienated into withdrawal from society. He is said to know it all, to be intelligent and amoral, well-mannered yet merciless, cynical in a young-old way, and oh so sophisticated. Some suburban youngsters are in flight from their own lives; others are deeply worried about what the future holds for them; and some are in revolt against their parents' suburban values.

At first glance most of our suburban youth share a common background of comfortable homes, loving parents, "good schools," high intelligence, excellent health, and almost unlimited opportunities for self-development. They have almost all the advantages that many of their mothers and fathers growing up during the Great Depression and World War II were denied. Yet many of today's middle-class suburban youngsters exhibit disturbing character qualities—sexual libertarianism, vehement rejection of adult authority, and a widespread disposition to experiment with drugs.[1]

Is the older generation really at fault? Or is this rebelling suburban generation the product of an overpermissive educational system? Are modern suburbia and its so-called

PHI DELTA KAPPAN, June 1969, pp. 575-578.

located in suburbia is not being cultivated in a manner essential to effective growth of democratic ideals; and there are now some real doubts emerging about the kinds of leadership suburban youth might someday contribute to our society.

Suburban Deprivation

Our nation's suburbias are evidently becoming so segregated that children can grow up without genuine contact with others of different racial, religious, or social backgrounds. The result is a growing provincialism in spite of ease of travel and communication. Suburbia's children are living and learning in a land of distorted values and faulty perceptions. They have only the slightest notion of others; they judge them on the basis of suburban standards (such as "cleanliness" and "niceness"), generalize about groups on the basis of the few they might have known, and think in stereotypes. In short, they usually have little association with or knowledge of people who differ in appearance or attitudes.

Dan Dodson, director of the Center for Human Relations and Community Studies at New York University, addressing himself to the problems facing youngsters living in suburban societies, declared: "In the suburbs a significant hardship on youngsters is their essential uselessness. They are 'kept' people well into their teens and often longer. There is little a youth can do to contribute to his family's well-being except to make top grades. But this contribution can go to a limited number only."[2]

Dodson further claims that there is considerable evidence that life in the suburbs is harder on boys than on girls. One reason is that the fathers are away from home so much of the time that their sons have only a vaguely conceptualized father-figure with which to identify.

Similarly, the values, attitudes, and behavior of older generation suburbanites are often exposed by the mass media as superficial and empty. For example, youthful critics of the middle-class suburban society vividly illustrated their rejection of suburbanite values in their acceptance of *The Graduate*, a film which devastatingly portrays the affluent, banal, swimming pool-and-corner-bar suburban set as seen through the eyes of its youthful "hero." The chief reason this film became such a social phenomenon is, perhaps, the forlorn manner in which the protagonist copes with the phoniness of a materially comfortable contemporary society. It says something about the meaninglessness of affluent life which distorts youthful aims and ambitions. It dramatizes the generation gap, portraying a youth almost paralyzed by the rapacious hedonism of his suburbanite parents.

Some authorities suggest that this alienation of the suburban child from "others" is a recent phenomenon stemming from the unique structure of suburban life. Discussing this idea, Goldman[3] uses the words *sidewalk* and *station wagon* as keys to understanding:

> The sidewalk [once] symbolized the avenue of communication between one child and another. In many areas this has vanished. . . . Sidewalks are no longer built . . . in some suburban housing developments. The response to the disappearing sidewalk is the mother-driven station wagon. Instead of relying

upon informal mingling of children, the image of the station wagon implies a planned, structured mingling of children: the Boy Scout meeting at 7:30, the Little League game at 4:00, the music lesson at 5:00, etc. What is gained by structuring common activities for children may be lost by some of the concomitant results—the loss of spontaneity when games and recreation must be carefully scheduled and supervised, the early creation of the "organization man," etc. The increased number of nursery schools is part of the same response to the deprivation of young children.

Other critics of contemporary suburban life have asserted that parents in suburbia pamper and spoil their children to such an extent that the children grow up without any real parental supervision. Halleck has declared that "some parents in suburbia have, through painstaking efforts to avoid creating neuroses in their children, abdicated their responsibility to teach and discipline their children. In so doing they have reared a generation of spoiled, greedy youth who are unable to tolerate the slightest frustration without showing an angry or infantile response."[4]

On the other hand, many critics put the blame for youthful unrest in suburbia on the way the children are overprotected and parentally dominated. This goes beyond an overabundance of material things. Rather, it consists of parental hovering and a reluctance to let their youngsters assume self-responsibility and self-direction. Perhaps some suburban parents fear their children will make mistakes and embarrass them. In any case, from an early age many suburban children are given little opportunity to use their own resources and make appropriate decisions.

Obviously, both extremes are unhealthy and undoubtedly contribute greatly to the restlessness and antisocial behavior patterns of rebelling suburban youth.

Of one thing we are sure, and that is that parental influence over suburban youth has deteriorated markedly; and children are cheated and deprived of experiences essential for effective development of wholesome ideals and attitudes. Unless more authentic human values are developed within our suburbias, the suburbian style of life will significantly contribute to the further deprivation of suburban youth. While little can be done about the attitudes and values inherited from parents, the schools still have the opportunity to reach these restless youth and redirect their energies. But first the challenge must be recognized.

Schools Share the Blame

"Suburban children are underprivileged. . . . There is little in their education, formal or otherwise, to familiarize them with the rich diversity of American life." This judgment by Alice Miel in *The Shortchanged Children of Suburbia*[5] grew out of a series of research studies designed to explore life in suburbia and to determine what is being taught about human differences in our schools. Her findings were alarming and resulted in a sharp indictment of the suburban school for failure to do something about preparing suburban children for a healthy, wholesome life in our society.

The results of this study indicate that:

- The typical suburban elementary school student's life is almost totally insulated and circumscribed.
- Suburban youngsters learn, individually, to be bigoted and hypocritical about racial, religious, economic, and ethnic differences at an early age.
- Group prejudices, too, take root early—and go deep.
- Materialism, selfishness, misplaced aggression, fake values, and anxiety top the list of common characteristics.

Yet many educators today are neither adequately trained nor perceptive enough to cope with the problems experienced by adolescents growing up in our affluent suburbs, and these inadequacies of staff hamper efforts to provide compensatory treatment.

For example, on the basis of some recent career pattern studies, it is now estimated that about 85 out of every 100 secondary school teachers in our suburban schools are from family backgrounds that differ markedly from those of the majority of the students in their classrooms. These teachers are said to undergo an emotional trauma when teaching suburban pupils. Problems of adaptation and adjustment are many. Faced with an "affluence" and "sophistication" (as doubtful as it may be) that they themselves might never have experienced, teachers in suburbia often expect and accept different standards of behavior. It stands to reason that by condoning these unique standards of behavior, teachers must bear some responsibility for the distorted values and attitudes as well as the antisocial behavior patterns often displayed by suburban youth.

Not only are some suburban educators not emotionally equipped to teach suburban youth—they may not be intellectually equipped either. "Many secondary school teachers have lower I.Q.'s than those of the suburban children they teach." This is what S. Alan Cohen of Yeshiva University said about suburban educators when he suggested that:

These teachers are unable to challenge their better students because they are afraid to. Many teachers are terrorized by the intellectual precocity of middle-class children. As a result, they cling tenaciously to rigid, lock-step pedagogies and mediocre materials to hold down the natural flow of intellectual curiosity.[6]

In asserting that suburban middle-class schools are not providing as good an education as they should, critic Cohen cites the growing evidence of educational inadequacy— the irrelevancy of curriculum content and the poor pedagogy—and concludes that superior test performances of children from "Scarsdales" tend to reflect the enriched verbal home environments rather than the school's educational program. "As a result," says Cohen, "the weak content and pedagogy in the middle-class schools are good enough, or perhaps more accurately, not bad enough to ruin these children."

Disappointingly enough, there are reports that school guidance counselors also experience difficulties when counseling in suburban schools. College counseling, for example, is theoretically only part of the total guidance function in secondary education. But in suburbia, college counseling becomes a major item of responsibility, and the counselor must become a master at it. Indeed, in the wealthy suburbs, where the citizenry have the money and desperately want to send their children to "good" colleges, they generally perceive counseling in "college" terms. Irvin Faust,[7] a suburban counselor, has written that:

> The trouble with most college-oriented communities and the counselors they hire is that college placement rather than welfare of students proves the guidance program; it becomes the total force rather than the natural result of a developmental counseling experience. . . . Whatever else arises is subordinate. He's awash in the suburban syndrome that says it's worse not to get into college than to flunk out. And it's worse not to get into a particular college, or colleges, for collecting acceptances is part of the game.

Suburban youths themselves have become progressively more sensitive to the lack of substance and meaning in the curriculum of their schools and are voicing strong concerns over the lack of relevancy. Many suburban youngsters, for example, are now said to be articulate, irreverent, humorless, and relentless in their contempt for what they honestly view as the meaninglessness of suburban education. They turn to one another when shaping beliefs or seeking advice, for they have learned to distrust both their parents and their teachers.

For some time now, the attentions and interests of most educators have been directed toward the educational problems relative to urban conditions of life. Recently, however, some concern has been given to shortcomings in rural education. But only little concern has been shown toward the possible needs of suburban youth, and the thought of any possible weakness in the education of suburbia's children has been virtually nonexistent. But the cultural circumstances of the suburbs are alive with challenges to the schools. Without compensatory approaches in the educational program, the suburban schools will fall far short of achieving the high purposes they are expected to achieve.

Compensatory Programs

Occasionally school officials and boards of education in affluent suburban communities are perceptive enough to grasp the defects of contemporary suburban life and commit themselves to some form of action. There have been some noteworthy attempts to revitalize the suburban curriculum and bring meaning and substance to instruction. One major illustration of this is the growing tendency among suburban schools to emphasize a human relations approach to instruction in the classroom.

Indeed, human relations programs hold promise for the future of suburban youngsters. Without instruction relative to the human environment in the suburban schools, many suburban youngsters will grow up with little chance for wholesome personal development. But setbacks do occur. In one well-known Buffalo suburban community—Williamsville, New York—the board of education backed away from a regional Title III project which would have sent a corps of teachers into its schools to improve instruction in human relations. The reason? A band of more than 100 citizens opposed the program, claiming "it would interfere with parents' lessons in human relations."[8] A sad day for Williamsville.

There are other programs suburban educators might seriously consider introducing in their schools if they would wish to see their students overcome the restrictive aspects of suburban life. Examples include:

• Instruction about different groups and cultures which could help eliminate prejudices and misconceptions about others. Personal experience with children of other groups can show a disadvantaged suburban youth directly, immediately, and concretely that not all members of a different group are "stupid, dirty, or dishonest." Suburban youths need supplementary reality experiences to make it possible for them to "see" society as it really is so that they may develop the empathy and compassion essential for the development of wholesome values and attitudes.

• More social, interscholastic, and subject-matter club activities in order to involve students in meaningful intergroup situations. Service clubs and school-community organizations serve as a very useful vehicle in relating the schooling process to community needs while restoring a sense of personal worth for our troubled suburban youth.

• Suburban schools should actively assist in fostering a return of the "family unit" by encouraging child-parent attendance at school functions. Rather than tol-erate parental isolation, the suburban schools must assist in creating a climate conducive to close family ties through school-centered activities, attempting primarily to entice fathers to share in these school events with their children.

• The schools of suburbia must expand the counseling staff at both the secondary and elementary levels. Individual and group counseling is imperative—especially in the elementary grades when attitudes are still malleable. After-school counseling with parents also seems essential, in view of the alarming increase in family conflicts occurring within the suburban communities.

• A major factor—perhaps the most important one—in providing suburban youth with direction and eliminating youthful prejudices is that of teacher attitudes.[9] Suburban educators must teach suburban youth with warmth, respect, and understanding. This, however, can only follow self-examination and insightful knowledge of the problems and pressures experienced by suburban youth. The attitudes of teachers about themselves and their relationships with and responsibilities to the suburban disadvantaged must first be clarified through in-service programs. Suburban teachers must develop a more comprehensive understanding of the nature of suburban life and its inherent defects.

• The schools should involve students more deeply in the task of teaching and curriculum construction, thereby serving two purposes: 1) determining just what aspects of the curriculum are indeed relevant from the student's point of view, and 2) improving the sense of worth of the student through responsible participation in the educational process. Why not have students contribute their views through the previewing of audio or visual materials; through examination of textbooks, library books, and other resource materials; through assisting in the instruction of slower or retarded children; through assuming leadership responsibilities in discussion groups and seminars? Why not delegate to the students more responsibility in designing school codes of conduct; supervision of study, library, or lunch areas; and enforcement of school discipline? Much could be gained—both by the schools and the students.

The defects of suburban society and the misconceptions brought by suburban students to the schools remain serious obstacles in the path of social progress. If the people of the suburbs—including suburbia's educators—would have their children grow up to respect all men and to seek for others the same scope of opportunity available to themselves, it is imperative that the suburban schools help develop the understandings and attitudes essential for constructive citizenship. Otherwise, the American Dream becomes the American Tragedy, and alienation and isolation become even more a way of life for youth trapped in their suburban environment.

[1]Yet Kenneth Keniston in *Notes On Committed Youth* (New York: Harcourt, Brace and World, 1968) asserts that these young radicals are unusually "healthy" youth who have solved their psychological problems to a higher degree than most and have achieved "an unusual degree of psychological integration." With respect to drug use, read "Scarsdale Seeks To Curb Use of Drugs," *New York Times*, January 27, 1969, and "Cause Shown," *American School Board Journal*, February , 1969, p. 5.

[2]Dan Dodson, "Are We Segregating Our Children?" *Parents Magazine*, September, 1963.

[3]Louis Goldman, "Varieties of Alienation and Educational Responses," *Teachers College Record*, January, 1968, pp. 331-44; Charles H. Harrison, "In the Suburbs," *Education News*, September, 1968, pp. 15, 19.

[4]S. L. Halleck, "Hypotheses of Student Unrest," PHI DELTA KAPPAN, September, 1968, pp. 2-9.

[5]Alice Miel and Edwin Kieste, *The Shortchanged Children of Suburbia*. New York: Institute of Human Relations Press, American Jewish Committee, 1967. It is interesting to contrast Miel's publication with the University of Chicago's recent study, *The Quality of Inequality: Urban and Suburban Public Schools* (Chicago: The University of Chicago Center for Public Study, 1968), the authors of which seem to feel that suburban schools are successful by any measure and provide the efforts necessary to offset deficiencies of environment. In all fairness, however, this title is misleading, for the book primarily examines the problems of urban education and only indirectly addresses itself to the defects of suburban schooling.

[6]S. Alan Cohen, "Local Control and the Cultural Deprivation Fallacy," PHI DELTA KAPPAN, January, 1969, pp. 255-59.

[7]Irvin Faust, "Guidance Counseling in Suburbia," *Teachers College Record*, February, 1968, pp. 449-58.

[8]"Suspect Negroes of Being Human," *Education News*, September 9, 1968.

[9]See *Report of the National Advisory Council on the Education of Disadvantaged Children*. Washington, D.C.: Government Printing Office, January 31, 1967.

PROFESSIONALISM

QUALITY
RESEARCH—

A Goal for Every Teacher

BYRON G. MASSIALAS
FREDERICK R. SMITH

PERIODIC reviews generally reveal that the volume of research conducted in elementary and secondary schools by school personnel is steadily increasing. Although one could not safely claim that we have reached our research peak, one could probably advance the proposition that classroom teachers are beginning to exhibit some interest in pursuing inquiries in their respective fields of specialization. In the social studies, for example, examination of some of the specialized journals will justify the latter statement.[1] Additional evidence can be found in bibliographies and reviews of research.[2]

Research must have a qualitative as well as a quantitative dimension, however, and here much remains to be done. By quality research we mean research which is planned and carried out under conditions which are educationally and experimentally sound. The matter of quality is primarily

[1] For example, see the volumes of *Social Education* and *Social Studies* for the last five years.
[2] Clarence D. Samford, *Social Studies Bibliography: Curriculum and Methodology*, Southern Illinois University Press, Carbondale, Illinois, 1959. Also see Richard E. Gross and William V. Badger, "Social Studies," in the *Encyclopedia of Educational Research*, pp. 1296-1319, edited by Chester W. Harris, Third Edition, The Macmillan Co., New York, 1960.

PHI DELTA KAPPAN, March 1962, pp. 253-256.

a question of research design. It logically follows, then, that the reporting of the findings and conclusions of a study is really incomplete unless accompanied by an explicit and perhaps even elaborate discussion of the method and frame of reference which governed the study. Many times in journal reports we see findings and claims concerning a variety of pupil outcomes attributed to certain variables (content or teacher). These frequently fail to indicate the strategy of attack and technique of investigation utilized in arriving at such findings. It is practically impossible to assess the end product of research when there is no statement about the methodological approach used.

The classroom teacher is in a key position to study the effect of new materials, methodology, and similar innovations upon the learning process. Yet no matter how research-minded he may be, he is apt to miss an opportunity for worthwhile basic investigation if he is not aware of the research potential of the situation. Even when research opportunities are recognized, the classroom teacher or even an entire department may fail to take into account some of the basic considerations crucial to quality research.

Let us assume, for example, that we are faculty members of a social studies department eager to embark on a research project.[3] Here are some of the questions which we could ask ourselves. There is little doubt that the consideration of these questions will have significant influence upon the strength of our investigation.

1. *What is our research philosophy? For what purpose do we intend to conduct research?*

A number of alternative responses, not necessarily mutually exclusive, can be anticipated. A justification of research for purposes of problem solving might be to meet a specific and immediate problem confronting us. For example, in view of the fact that students are currently showing concern with fall-out and atomic radiation, or with the implications of our Berlin policy, how can we provide a new educational experience

[3] The social studies were selected for illustrative purposes only. The authors assume that these questions and the considerations which they imply are basic to research in most subject areas.

which would allow them to discuss these and related problems in a thoughtful manner? Could this problem be better met by creating a "current events club," or would it be more profitable to discuss such issues in regular classes?

On the other hand, a department might want to conduct research because of a long-range problem, i.e., since 90 per cent of our graduates continue their education in college, what kind of social studies curriculum should we be offering? Should we include anthropology and social psychology or should we concentrate on history? What would be the best way of selecting content from a vast body of socio-economic data? Should we try to introduce a seminar at the senior level for the purpose of familiarizing our mature students with social science research tools and techniques?

The attitude of the school administration and the community itself may set limitations or offer encouragement to classroom investigation and experimentation. Thus we might legitimately ask ourselves what the prevailing attitude is toward studies such as we contemplate. What is more important is a determination that we as a department will take a position as curriculum leaders in our subject field while simultaneously working toward the creation of an atmosphere which will be conducive to research and possible curricular innovation.

Professional growth can be offered as an additional incentive for research activity. Through participation in research the teacher may become interested in readings about his subject and new approaches to teaching and learning; he could find himself involved in curriculum meetings, lectures, conventions, and summer workshops. Furthermore, research can provide a climate whereby communication and exchange of ideas and teamwork are made possible not only for members within one faculty but also among several faculties. A spirit of scholarly competition and drive to excel might be the justification and the outcome of such inquiry.

Finally and most significantly, one could justify research on its own merit. That is, our research could contribute to the building of a systematic body of social studies theory. Here, for example, a faculty could discuss and investigate basic philosophies appropriate to social studies instruction and research, conceptualization concerning logical operations employed in the act of teaching, or elements which could be operationally identifiable in the decision-making process in the classroom. The purpose of this approach is to accurately classify and systematize social studies knowledge. The ultimate ends are explanatory. Usually in pure research there are no immediate pay-off considerations, although many times there are measurable and tangible outcomes. We must remember that since Ptolemy it has taken many generations of scientists to build up, slowly and painstakingly, a satisfactory theory of our solar system; finally, one individual, Copernicus, published his thesis of a heliocentric universe in 1543.[4]

2. *What are some fruitful areas of investigation in the social studies? Considering our limitations and resources, what can we do productively?*

Here a number of considerations demand further discussion and analysis. For example, a team of teachers might desire to study the daily activities in the social studies classroom. Paradoxically enough, although many investigators have conducted research in the social studies, very few have dealt with actual happenings at the purely descriptive level. It seems only logical to assume that unless we can conclusively respond to the "what is" question we cannot intelligently proceed with questions of "why" and "how."

Teachers will also have to assess their strengths and weaknesses concerning the research process. Major weak spots are, generally, the following: (1) lack of background and formal preparation in the statistical and measurement procedures in education; (2) certain limitations in time and/or ability to pursue studies that go beyond the confines of the classroom, i.e., follow-up studies; (3) heavy teaching loads and extracurricular responsibilities. On the other hand, the classroom teacher also has a number of advantages appropriate to the conduct of quality research: (1) He has direct contact with the

[4] For an elaborate statement concerning the value of basic research, see Nicholas A. Fattu, "The Teacher and Educational Research," *High School Journal* 44:194-203, March, 1961.

pupil and a knowledge of his problems, his intellectual potential, his socio-emotional development, and the like. (2) He is able to record happenings in the classroom and to put them in proper perspective as they affect the teaching-learning process. (3) He can, with certain limits, manipulate the educational environment and observe the corresponding reactions of the pupils.

In addition, the faculty will have to consider some seemingly unimportant yet indispensable factors, such as availability of physical facilities and equipment, space for trained observers, and the like. This is not to imply that quality experimentation demands excessively expensive equipment of facilities. It is only realistic, however, to evaluate these factors in terms of their appropriateness to the over-all design of the study.

3. *What is the domain of inquiry? How do we delimit our problem?*

Acknowledging the fact that there is interrelatedness in nature, we realize that we need to reduce the problem to one which is manageable and operationally definable. For certain objectives, perhaps, global views are necessary and important. But for our purposes as classroom teachers we need to be selective; thus we attempt systematically to delimit our sphere of investigation.

A five-year research project conducted at the University of Illinois under the auspices of the United States Office of Education identified three domains of inquiry in the classroom: the linguistic, the expressive, and the performative. The first referred to the verbal intercourse that takes place in the classroom. The second referred to the behavior of children as expressed through certain signs, facial or others. The last referred to behavior centered on demonstration or performance of certain tasks associated with laboratory work. Although all these domains were identified, Smith chose to investigate only the linguistic in terms of logical operations involved in the act of teaching.[5]

[5] B. Othanel Smith, *A Study of the Logic of Teaching: The Logical Structure of Teaching and the Development of Critical Thinking.* A Report of the First Phase of a Five-Year Research Project, Bureau of Educational Research, College of Education, University of Illinois, 1959. (Dittoed.) Also see, by the same author, "How Can You Help the Student Teacher Become a Real Teacher?" *Teacher College Journal* 32:15-21, October, 1960.

Bloom[6] and his associates, in an effort to classify and systematize educational objectives, identified three main domains: the cognitive, the affective, and the manipulative. The first included those objectives normally associated with knowledge, intellectual abilities, and skills. The second referred to objectives associated with interests, values, attitudes, preferences, adjustment, etc. The last included aspects of motor skill development. After he had operationally distinguished among the foregoing domains, he proceeded to investigate the first.

4. What philosophical and psychological rationale are we employing? What constructs do we want to use?

What assumptions appear to be warranted in planning our research? What postulates and propositions are we taking for granted? Are we going to accept Smith's[7] proposition that the act of teaching is related to but distinct from the act of learning? Does teaching involve a set of operations which could be logically and empirically discernible? Is it possible to categorize linguistic discourse in the social studies classroom? Can we assume, as Bruner[8] has stated, that there is an inherent "structure" underlying each discipline and subject matter area? Are we going to accept one particular theory of learning as valid and reliable and thus try to evaluate student behavior in such a light? Will we accept a connectionist theory of learning or a field theory as being most appropriate for achieving the desired outcomes in our subject area?

5. What is our unit of measurement? What strategies and techniques could we utilize?

Typical of the questions we might ask are the following: Would an existing standardized test provide an adequate measuring instrument? Do we need to construct our own evaluative instruments? If we are to measure or assess verbal exchange, what kind of measurement device can we apply?

Can we rely on teacher or student daily logs or anecdotal records as part of our evaluative de-

[6] Benjamin S. Bloom, editor, *Taxonomy of Educational Objectives*, Longmans, Green and Co., New York, 1956.
[7] Smith, *op. cit.*
[8] Jerome S. Bruner, *The Process of Education*, Harvard University Press, Cambridge, 1960.

sign?[9] Would we need some additional objective evidence for purposes of validating our instruments? Can we use tapes and video-tapes to maintain a permanent record of our investigation in the classroom? Will it be desirable to hire trained observers to visit our classrooms and record activities using, perhaps, a time-sampling technique? Can we justify one approach or technique over another within the total project and its underlying rationale?

6. *In what aspects of this research would we need help from a specialist?*

A faculty ready to initiate a research project will have to determine what kind of professional, expert help it will need. For example, if we are utilizing standardized tests, or even tests constructed by individual researchers for specific purposes, we would need assistance in tabulating the scores and in determining whether the instruments are valid and reliable. We may need advice on the selection of statistical techniques which will enable us to determine whether outcomes are statistically significant, or whether our purported correlations are indeed positive. We may need to consider the possibility of consulting with a specialist in the content area to attest to the reliability of certain propositions and key concepts that we are using in our teaching.

7. *How do we evaluate and confirm our procedures and findings?*

Here we are mainly concerned with the validity of our product. We might be thinking in terms of replication and follow-up studies which will provide the necessary justification of our propositions. In this connection we might want to refine our procedures and investigate techniques as we proceed with our study. Ryans'[10] seven year project in teacher competence is an example of untiring devotion to obtain a logical and empirical confirmation of findings through an exhaustive attempt at the refinement of research tools and a continuous search for reconstruction of generalizations.

[9] For an analysis of promising new techniques in conducting research in the social studies see Byron G. Massialas, *Research Prospects in the Social Studies*, in the *Bulletin* of the School of Education, Indiana University, Vol. 38, No. 1, January, 1962.

[10] David G. Ryans, *Characteristics of Teachers*, Council on Education, Washington, D. C., 1960.

Summary

At the fingertips of the classroom teacher lie innumerable opportunities for research which may be the source of additional insight into many of the problems of understanding the teaching-learning process. While we must operate within the limits set by the nature of our teaching assignment, level of training in research techniques, and necessary content background, the teacher should and can become capable of conducting quality research. Among the principal points of justification for such endeavors, professional growth, problem solving, and systematic theory building are especially worthy of consideration. But whatever purpose the research is to serve, a statement of the underlying philosophy and rationale is indispensable. A systematic, thoughtful, and vigorous approach to the investigation is necessary if we are to expect a clear design and a valid strategy of attack. Only when tight and organized frames of reference are consciously employed will the field of education move toward quality research.

163

The New Teacher and Interpersonal Relations in the Classroom [1]

HELENE BORKE

JOAN W. BURSTYN

Often a successful teacher can by the very strength of his personality carry students as a group with him through the curriculum. This is the teacher who is "born, not made." However, with the growing emphasis on learning rather than teaching and on individual rather than group activities, this kind of success is no longer so important. Today, a teacher needs to be successful in understanding and guiding the individual student.

Understanding means more than merely being nice to a student. It entails mastering skills in interpersonal behavior that should be available to prospective teachers as soon as they begin classroom teaching; the best-intentioned teacher may quickly become disillusioned if his attempts to understand a student are met with derision or scorn. This paper is an analysis of the effects of a seminar in interpersonal relations provided for several groups of student teachers while they were doing their teaching practice. In this short period, seminar members established relationships with their classes and developed an understanding of individual students that teachers seldom acquire without years of experience. Some student teachers reported dramatic changes of attitude that affected their behavior outside as well as inside the classroom.

A number of factors appeared responsible for these results. The students perceived teaching practice as a frontier experience; each faced situations he had not visualized before that challenged his view of himself and made him receptive to new ideas. The seminar provided him with

1. The first seminars in interpersonal relations in the classroom held at Carnegie-Mellon University were supported by a grant from the Maurice Falk Medical Fund, Pittsburgh. The authors would like to thank Sylvia Farnham-Diggory, John Sandberg, and Stonewall Stickney, M.D., for their assistance as consultants, and Erwin Steinberg for his many helpful suggestions.

JOURNAL OF TEACHER EDUCATION (AACTE), 1970, Vol. 21, pp. 378-381.

methods he could use at once for handling his problems. The success experienced with first attempts at problem solving motivated students to experiment further with new approaches in relating to individual students and to the class as a whole.

The close relationship among members in each seminar, and between each member and the leader, was also crucial to the success of the seminars. Members did not want gripe sessions, nor were they helped much by hearing that others had the same problems. They did want individual conferences with the leader, after which they were prepared to share their experiences with other members of the seminar.

Another factor making for success was the variety of experiences provided in the seminar. Students did not agree on which was the most valuable: some felt it was the diaries; some, the videotapes; some, the sharing of experiences; and others, the focused exercises. In all cases, however, the value lay in a growing ability to assess one's own experiences and to help others assess theirs. The group leaders were not supervisors or critics; rather, they provided interpersonal resource material and helped to foster a supportive environment for individual experimentation.

Four main topics relating to interpersonal behavior were presented in the seminars:

1. *Problem solving as an effective approach for improving interpersonal communication.* The success of the seminars depended on the participants' acceptance of this approach. At first, some were reluctant to apply problem-solving techniques to the field of personal relationships; they felt threatened by the possibility of alternative forms of response, particularly in the classroom, where their authority could easily be undermined. Some were unwilling to experiment because they felt unsure of their skill. Yet, in the end, they all began to experiment with new ways of behaving to individual students and to rely on feedback from students' behavior for deciding which behavior patterns were the most satisfactory. An effective beginning proved to be the diaries of interpersonal incidents kept by group members. At first, some members were not able to isolate such incidents, but when asked to concentrate on incidents involving one or two students only, or themselves and their critic teacher, they were soon able to do so. Sometimes, role playing was introduced as a way to try out alternative forms of response to a given situation.

2. *Phenomenology, or the awareness that each individual has his own idiosyncratic ways of perceiving the world.* Each individual is genetically unique and has had unique experiences in life. The way he feels and thinks at any particular moment will affect the way he perceives what is happening, and his perception will, in turn, affect his behavior. In the seminars, the implications for teaching of differences in perception were explored: how a teacher has to develop empathy with his students, since it is crucial for reciprocal communication. Also analyzed was the effect of trying to relate to other people on the basis of their external characteristics instead of getting to know them as individuals. What were the possible categories into which teachers might place their students, and students their teachers? The most obvious related to sex, social class, and color; others were such common categories as troublemaker

and show-off. Members then examined their relationships with two students —one with whom they got on well and one with whom they were having difficulty—to see in what ways they might be categorizing the students as a result of their perception of the students' behavior.

3. *Interrelationship of the cognitive and interpersonal aspects of the learning experience.* People learn most effectively when they are motivated to learn. Part of this motivation is related to the content of what is taught (e.g., its relevance), but part is related to a person's perception of himself as someone capable of learning. As John Holt[2] has pointed out so poignantly, our schools are expert at reinforcing inadequacy. The more inadequate a student feels, the less motivated he becomes; the less motivated he becomes, the less good his work, the lower his grade, and the more inadequate he feels. The problem, then, is to break this series of interactions. By raising the question of grades within the larger framework of personal adequacy, it was possible to get seminar members to focus on the crucial role of the teacher in helping each student to develop positive feelings about himself and his ability to learn.

4. *Nonverbal behavior as an aspect of interpersonal communication.* Alerting members to the implications of nonverbal behavior proved to be a most valuable experience for them. Smiling, frowning, eye contact, a touch on shoulder or arm, even the angle of the head while listening, all were explored by members in connection with classroom behavior. Videotapes were especially helpful for examining this

2. Holt, John. *How Children Fail.* New York: Pitman Publishing Corp., 1964.

type of behavior, since members were able to go back over tapes to view again significant movements by their students and themselves.

To summarize, it is felt that the student-teaching experience is the best time to introduce a seminar in interpersonal relations. Since many students experience at this time a personal crisis that is frequently severe, they search for new ways to cope (2) and, consequently, are probably more receptive to new ideas and more willing to try new ways of relating to people than they are later on in their careers.

The model selected for this seminar was the human relations laboratory. The basic assumptions of laboratory training are that new concepts about human relations arise from immediate emotional experiences rather than from abstract discussions about them and that such experiences provide the concrete reference point to which theories concerning human behavior can be related (1, 5). Experiences of group members in their teaching practice were used as one reference point and their experiences in the seminars as another. Through focused exercises, diaries, and videotapes, it was possible to provide the students with an opportunity to become participant-observers of their own behavior. This kind of seminar appears to be ideally suited for developing in teachers an understanding of the importance of interpersonal relations in the classroom.

References

1. Bradford, Leland P.; Gibb, Jack R.; and Benne, Kenneth D., editors. *T-Group Theory and Laboratory Method: Innovation in Re-education.* New York: Wiley, 1964.
2. Caplan, Gerald. *Principles of Preventive*

Psychiatry. New York: Basic Books, 1964.

3. Fox, Robert; Luszki, Margaret; and Schmuck, Richard. *Diagnosing Classroom Learning Environments.* Chicago: Science Research Associates, 1966.

4. Koff, Robert H. "Classroom Dynamics and Teacher Training." *The Journal of Teacher Education* 20: 57-60; Spring 1969.

5. Schein, Edgar H., and Bennis, Warren G. *Personal and Organizational Change Through Group Methods: The Laboratory Approach.* New York: Wiley, 1965.

6. Schmuck, Richard A. "Helping Teachers Improve Classroom Group Processes." *Journal of Applied Behavioral Science* 4: 401-35; October/November/December 1968.

WHO SHALL BE THE
EFFECTIVE VOICE FOR AMERICAN TEACHERS?

K. Forbis Jordan
Assistant Executive Secretary
Indiana School Boards Association

THE great challenge to public education as we know it today is not in the curricular areas; it is not the increasing demands for the tax dollar; it is not frills in buildings or the nature of professional courses for teachers. Rather, the challenge is in the rapidly developing conflict between the National Education Association and the American Federation of Teachers. Which of these two bodies will become the effective voice for the teachers of America?

Assuming that the NEA with its resources, prestige, and image does win the battle and gain sufficient members to represent the teachers in the large urban centers, what will be the result? What impact will the battle have on the children in the classrooms of America? Will their opportunities be better, or will they become mere pawns in the struggle for numbers by these two giant organizations? Will the "accident of birth" cliché which is often heard as defense for federal aid also apply to those unfortunate children who attended schools placed under sanctions by the NEA or one of its affiliates? Will the end justify the means, or will the professional rise to the occasion and remember the reason for his existence?

Few would question that the professional teacher deserves a living wage, one which recognizes that portion of his life which has been devoted to preparation and experience. The question which concerns many people is the method which should be used to obtain the just remuneration which the professional teacher deserves.

In this entire ideological conflict the local school board finds itself caught in the middle; there are factors which influence the decisions of the board which are not found in many other employee–employer relationships. Being a governmental agency with limited powers, but definite responsibilities, the local school board must do everything within its powers to provide the best possible educational program within the socio-cultural and economic climate of a given school district. Wide variations in tax structure and in state support programs coupled with local school district philosophies and values have resulted in correspondingly wide variations in educational opportunities both within and between individual states. School boards in a given community must operate within this legal and philosophical framework. As teachers become a profession with self governing and regulatory powers, can local school boards retain their role and fulfill their function? As teachers unite and become a powerful force at the local, state, and national levels, will school districts be forced to seek means of counteracting this force? Will local school districts be forced to unite, or will the state legislatures become more actively involved in the educational process by assuming powers delegated to local districts?

Many observers contend that one of the things which has helped our educational system to experience its tremendous growth is the base of control of the American public schools. As teachers organize more effectively on a nationwide basis, will local school districts be able to continue to operate as they do at the present time? Local school boards in their policymaking functions have greatly contributed to the progress which has been made by the innovators and the dreamers who have brought about many of the educational advances which have been made in the past several years. If school boards cannot continue to operate effectively and are forced to unite into a more potent organization, local boards will have to sacrifice some individuality as they seek greater power.

Regardless of the choice that teachers make, it appears that our schools are on the road to becoming "closed shops." Professional negotiations seem rather mild when compared with collective bargaining and arbitration; however, there is little difference in the end result if local school districts are unable to secure teachers because of sanctions imposed by the local, state, or national association. Presently, all eyes are turned toward Utah where the possibility of sanctions for the entire state looms. If successful sanctions can be imposed on an entire state, the alternatives available to the local school district will be limited when the school board is faced with a professional staff which is dissatisfied with the conditions of employment as they exist. They can do little but yield to the pressure unless some new alternative appears.

Future state legislatures may find themselves more directly involved in the problems which face the schools. The choice of statewide salary schedules or compulsory arbitration may be in the offing. Arbitration procedures have already been established in some states. If the problems cannot be resolved, representatives from the two interested parties meet with a third party; this group then recommends to the school board. The school board may accept or reject the recommendation. Both the teachers and school board have yielded some of their control when it becomes necessary to submit to this procedure.

Another and possibly a more paternalistic approach is that the local school board has responsibility for operating the schools and developing the educational philosophy which serves as a guideline for the schools, this philosophy having been developed in line with the wishes and desires of the community. Teachers coming to any community have an opportunity to make their decision concerning employment in the community in light of the local educational philosophy. If local school boards are permitted to continue to operate in this manner, the people will continue to reap the benefits from a state system of education operated at the local level. If this approach is to be accepted, teachers must accept a responsibility within the community, make themselves heard, and be a positive force for the multiple aspects of public education.

Lay control of public education is at stake throughout the nation; the problem is more acute in certain sections than in other. Salaries are not the only items under consideration; textbooks, curricular decisions, working conditions, and other factors are as important as salaries. The basic question is whether or not teacher organizations and school boards are willing to sincerely attempt to solve their problems at the local level and are willing to accept and abide by whatever decision may be reached. If not, is each group going to look to a more powerful agency outside the community, and in doing so abdicate some of its power and individuality? Simply, man is again faced with a challenge in the recurring problem area of human relations. Can two men, or two groups of men, set face to face, examine a problem, and arrive at a mutually acceptable solution without calling for assistance?

UNIONISM VERSUS PROFESSIONALISM IN TEACHING

RICHARD D. BATCHELDER

INFORMED citizens throughout the United States are becoming increasingly aware of the struggle between organized labor and the independent professional associations for the allegiance of the public school teachers of America. This is not merely a struggle between two rival teaching groups—the American Federation of Teachers and the NEA—but between opposing concepts about teaching and public education.

It is impossible to overemphasize the importance of this struggle, for the outcome may well determine the future course of public education and of our nation's progress. All citizens, not only teachers, have a stake in this struggle, whether they think so or not.

The fundamental issue is not the contribution of the American labor movement to our economy and our society. The NEA is not antilabor: it is opposed only to labor's control of the schools. The fundamental issue, therefore, is the union approach to teaching and to public education versus the professional approach.

THE American Federation of Teachers has been in existence since 1916, but until recently it enrolled few teachers. In fact, in 1961 Myron Lieberman, a writer on educational topics and an erstwhile candidate for the presidency of the AFT, characterized the organization as:

. . . seriously deficient both as a professional organization and as a union. The AFT has no real program in certification, accreditation, or professional ethics. Its journal is nothing but a house organ, and most of its publications are propagandistic in nature. . . .

TODAY'S EDUCATION—NEA JOURNAL, April 1966, pp. 18-20.

171

In the last five years, the AFT has gained some 60,000 members while NEA has gained over 200,-000. Even now after hundreds of thousands of dollars have been poured into AFT organizing of teachers by the Industrial Union Department of AFL-CIO, less than 6 percent of America's teachers are members of the teachers union.

During the current school year, professional associations have won practically all the contests for representation. For example, associations in Connecticut have won 22 of 23 elections; associations in Michigan have won 411 of 426 elections or stipulations [recognition by the school board on the basis of verified majority membership]; and in the state of Washington, by an overall margin of more than 20 to 1, local education associations have been designated exclusive representatives in over 40 elections as compared to one union victory.

During 1964-65, the AFT increased its membership by about 10 percent, adding some 10,400 members to a total of some 100,000 enrolled previously. AFT's drive to represent increasing numbers of American teachers is costly: Approximately 40 percent of its 1964-65 budget was devoted to "organizing and servicing" new memberships.

The recent stepped-up campaign of the AFT to attract teachers is made possible by large sums of money pumped into it, primarily by the Industrial Union Department of AFL-CIO, which contains such major unions as the United Auto Workers, the United Steel Workers, and the International Association of Machinists.

During the 1960's, the American Federation of Teachers has served as a spearhead for the AFL-CIO, in general, and its IUD, in particular, in a drive to unionize white collar workers and professionals.

According to its financial report for the two and to act at all times as they teach—honorably and responsibly. The NEA will continue to ask that teachers conduct themselves so as to protect the interests of the students and the public as well as their own interests.

INDEPENDENCE for the teaching profession is essential because public education is for all people and support for public education comes from all segments of society. Although professional education associations have often been able to improve their services to teachers and to education by working closely with other groups—including segments of organized labor—they have jealously guarded their independence.

By contrast, the United Federation of Teachers, the AFT's largest affiliate, states in its constitution that its first objective is "to cooperate to the fullest extent with the labor movement and to work for a progressive labor philosophy; to awaken in all teachers a labor consciousness and a sense of solidarity with labor."

At the annual convention of the New Mexico State AFL-CIO last year, Herrick Roth, president of the Colorado Labor Council and a vice-president of the AFT, was quoted by the *Albuquerque Tribune* as saying that the labor movement will not reach its ultimate in America until "union shop signs are hanging in every classroom."

Teachers certainly must discuss the labor movement and its contributions to American society. Trade unions have had an important role in the industrial world. But union members owe their basic allegiance to the overall labor movement and shape their policies to its requirements; teachers cannot gear their teaching to the dictates of any special interest group—whether it be a labor group, a business enterprise, or a political party.

Allied formally with the labor movement, teachers would be under pressure to relinquish their freedom and adhere to labor's point of view on specific issues.

How the education profession is organized is *not* a struggle between comparable contenders. It is profoundly important to understand the significant difference between teachers organized in unions and teachers organized in independent professional groups. The freedom and independence of the educational process are at stake. The outcome will affect the public as well as the teachers.

The inability of organized labor to win recent National Labor Relations Board elections has been blamed in part on the failure of teachers to indoctrinate high school students with the importance of the labor movement. Speaking at the 1963 AFT convention, Nicholas Zonarich of the IUD called upon teachers to expand educational instruction relative to unionism among young people now in high school.

The NEA opposes efforts of any group in society years ending June 30, 1965, the IUD allocated $362,000 for the AFT's organizing drive. This was in addition to funds coming from other union sources. For example, in 1965 the New York City Transit Workers Union gave $25,000 to the organizing fund of the United Federation of Teachers, the AFT local in New York.

Labor's sudden interest in organizing teachers was explained in a *New York Times* article of December 19, 1965, which noted that the number of workers belonging to unions had declined from a peak of nearly 17.5 million in 1956 to a little more than 16.8 million by the end of 1964. The article continued:

Whether the AFL-CIO will be able . . . to end this plight remains to be seen. . . . Optimists believe they already see the signs of a stirring. They point out that there has been a rapid rise lately in unionization of government workers, for instance. And, they are particularly pleased by the sharp climb in the organization of teachers, which they hope will break down the white collar workers' hostility toward unions.

Organized labor is actively recruiting teachers to maintain or increase its numerical strength. It seeks teachers as a necessary stepping-stone to the unionization of millions of technical and white collar workers in government, the new space industries, and business.

Basic disagreement between the NEA and the AFT may be concisely stated in two words: responsibility and independence.

The NEA has counseled responsible action on the part of the teaching profession. It has asked its members to honor their contractual obligations to further its own ends at the expense of sound, objective teaching in our schools. The curriculum must serve the needs of children—not the needs of any special interest group.

But labor does not intend teachers to be independent. Its leaders expect teachers to serve labor's cause. This policy was reiterated last year at the forty-ninth annual AFT convention by President Cogen, who said:

Every AFT member knows the practical need for making sure that our brothers and sisters in other unions are there when we need them. They will be ready to help us if we are "there" when they need *our* support.

What happens when teachers assume obligations which cause them to take actions which are incompatible with their own or their students' best interests? In Illinois, members of the Granite City teachers union voted not to cross the picket line in a strike by janitors and cafeteria workers in April 1964.

In Cleveland, the teachers union, acting on behalf of other unions, urged the school board to refrain from purchasing textbooks and other materials printed by Kingsport Press, which is involved in an unfair labor practices dispute with various printing unions. Acting upon the union's recommendations, the Cleveland school board passed the following resolution unanimously: "The superintendent is instructed to not place bulk purchases from the Kingsport Press without first reporting to the Board on the circumstances of the strike."

Kingsport prints books for some of the most reputable and largest textbook publishers in the country. The quality or suitability of the textbooks and other materials is not at issue; the dispute involves other unions not primarily concerned with the education of children. Nevertheless, the AFT has called for member locals throughout the country to ask school boards to refrain from purchasing books printed by this one company.

Although the NEA appreciates the feelings of members of the unions at Kingsport, the Association insists that the chief criteria for the use or non-use of books and other instructional materials in public schools are their educational value and appropriateness. The teaching profession must not become embroiled in secondary boycotts arising from labor disputes.

INDEPENDENCE also is an important issue in the financing of public education. As the voice of the independent teaching profession, NEA and its affiliates have always supported a flexible tax structure which will provide adequate support for public education.

Teachers unions, however, are strongly influenced by labor policy, which generally opposes the levying of certain types of taxes, particularly sales taxes. In some places, this has resulted in union teachers' opposing the enactment of the very taxes that were meant to increase support for public education, including much needed salary increases for teachers.

In Indiana, for example, legal action by the AFL-CIO in 1963 delayed for almost four months the collection of an already-enacted sales tax that was designed to provide badly needed funds for public education. The state lost $39 million in tax collections. The loss for schools was equivalent to $650 per instructional unit. As a result, thousands of pupils were without instructional materials and supplies they should have had, and teachers failed to receive deserved salary increases.

Organized labor also fought tax measures that would have provided increased support for the schools in California, Maryland, Pennsylvania, Ohio, Kentucky, and Louisiana.

NEA believes that it is the responsibility of the teaching profession to make the case for adequate school support and to press for revenues from any legitimate source available.

This is of special importance because the graduated federal income tax has become the source of support for the expanding activities of the federal government. This leaves in most cases the sales tax as the only remaining source available to the state legislatures which is productive enough to provide revenues needed to support the schools.

To refuse sales tax revenues in many states is tantamount to denying the only source capable of serving school needs.

By affiliating with the AFL-CIO, the teachers union must sometimes subordinate its own objectives to those of its parent body. The NEA is unwavering in its belief that teachers must be free to make their own decisions based upon their professional objectives.

The objectives of the independent professional associations are to promote excellence in the work

176

of educators, to generate public support for education, and to protect and advance the interests of members and students. This course serves the entire American society, not merely one special interest group, and at the same time serves teachers.

We in the professional associations hold that teaching is unique among all professions. As a professional group, teachers must understand and interpret all facets of American life; they must remain free from any obligations or alliances that might result in conflict with the best interests of education. Teachers must remain responsible, independent, and free to teach, so that children may be free to learn.

A Talk
with
Albert Shanker

Donald W. Robinson

A LBERT SHANKER, relaxed, soft-spoken father of four, looks more like the philosophy professor he started out to be than the militant union leader he is. He reflects a quiet dedication to the cause he adopted 15 years ago when financial pressures led him to interrupt his doctoral studies in philosophy (including a teaching assistantship with Charles Frankel) and accept a long-term substitute job in the New York City schools.

Shanker is proud that one of the little-noticed provisions of his hard-won strike settlement last September specifies that the board will cease giving substitute licenses. "Furthermore," he says, "there is a penalty clause attached. If the board should continue to give substitute examinations after a certain date it would be required to place all substitutes on the appropriate salary schedule and pay other benefits and penalties to the tune of somewhere between $30 million and $50 million."

Almost immediately upon assuming his teaching duties Shanker became interested in teacher organization. He admits that his mother's involvement with the Garment Workers' Union had created a family environment favorable to unions. Not surprisingly, this atmosphere continues. Recently Shanker's five-year-old son, asked to identify George Washington, promptly replied, "He was the first president of the United Federation of Teachers."

The immediate condition that fed and has continued to feed Shanker's union zeal was the way New York teachers were treated. At the outset he objected to their being ordered to sacrifice part of their lunch periods for "snow duty." The objection was met with a curt, "You're lucky you have a job at all." Shanker admits that he dared to be bold because he had no intention of staying.

At this time (1952) New York City teachers were represented by

PHI DELTA KAPPAN, January 1968, pp. 255-266.

106 competing organizations. Shanker saw the need for teacher unity and he believed in the union concept. The achievement of that unity within the union has been a 15-year accomplishment to which he has been a major contributor. This has meant unending negotiation among teachers themselves. All 106 groups are now within the fold, and all competing interests must be reconciled.

That the union has achieved unity Shanker does not doubt. He says, "If there ever needs to be a stoppage in the future we can do it without pickets, without written resignations, without a strike vote. Two years from now if the contract is rejected by a majority of teachers, 50,000 teachers will just stay home, without being told by the leadership or by anybody else. We have our weapon for future use; it is individual teacher commitment."

Actually, the teacher resignations were never submitted during the September stoppage. Shanker had every intention of submitting them, but was dissuaded when a deputy superintendent threatened to turn men's names over to draft boards.

Shanker sees no evidence at all that a damaging public image of the teacher as a law-evader has been created, or that student idealism has suffered. Any student reaction, he believes, is very temporary. At the same time, the imperturbable president of the UFT does expect (as of October 25) that he will have to serve at least 10 days in jail.

If Shanker is pleased with the contract provision eliminating the substitute teacher, he is even more pleased with the proviso that insures an additional $10 million for experimental programs. Five million of this will finance additional intensive effort in elementary schools serving disadvantaged areas, including the controversial More Effective Schools (MES).

Shanker explained the origin of the MES schools, concerning which conflicting evaluations have been submitted. When Bernard Donovan was acting superintendent, he says, Donovan proposed that $2 million be set aside to provide $1,000 premiums for each of 2,000 teachers serving in "intolerable" schools. The union dubbed this hike "combat pay" and successfully opposed it. The acting superintendent then proposed the "Effective Schools" plan, with smaller classes. When the board objected to the implication that other schools were ineffective, the name was changed to *More* Effective Schools. When the cost was estimated at $1,200 per pupil, Donovan opposed the plan on the ground that the city could not afford it.

A little later, Superintendent Calvin Gross, under pressure from the union and the community, sanctioned the first 10 MES schools. A year later 11 more were added. Shanker asserts that teachers and pupils share the union's enthusiasm for the plan, and he predicts the continuation and expansion of the program or another like it.

Asked for his reactions to talk of an NEA-AFT merger, the UFT president expressed his disbelief that this could happen in the next few years. "It is impossible," he said, "for the NEA to make the necessary structural changes. The

NEA is too rigid. Their elections are closed affairs. Our elections are wide open. When Carl Megel was elected UFT president, a shift of 15 votes in the convention would have beaten him. Charles Cogen won by 16 votes. The delegates control the AFT convention, but this cannot be said of the NEA."

The conversation turned back to the benefits gained by the New York strike. "The salary gains are fantastic, with 25 percent of our teachers receiving take-home increases of $2,300 over a two-year period, and no one gaining less than $1,500. In addition we won valuable fringe benefits. Extra-duty activities—moonlighting, if you wish—will be paid for at the median salary for classroom teachers, which during this contract period will be $10.25 per hour. This agreement will benefit 20,000 of New York's 55,000 teachers. For the first time we have established the principle that a teacher's time is just as valuable after school as it is during the school day. This rate will apply to after-school recreation programs, to summer school work, and to other programs.

"We also had an expansion of our welfare fund this year. I think most teachers fail to realize that New York City teachers have a completely paid health plan covering major medical expenses. They have a dental plan for the entire family. They can walk into any of 3,000 drugstores and have any prescription filled for 75 cents. They can get a free pair of eyeglasses for each member of the family every two years. This year we got a $50 per teacher addition to the welfare fund. We expect to use most of that $50 for college scholarships for children of teachers within the school system. And this will be another first. I do not think that such benefits—these welfare benefits and these scholarship benefits—will very long remain a secret, and I think teachers in other districts will be demanding the same thing.

"It is also a clear gain that teachers in our special service elementary schools and in our ghetto schools will have a daily preparation period, and every two out of three years each junior high and senior high school teacher will have 10 unassigned periods a week, which is double the number they previously had. We accomplished this by eliminating the amount of time the principal can assign teachers to routine chores within the school.

"Finally, I would say that the stoppage showed a virtually new relationship between the city administration and the Board of Education. The Board of Education really is dead; it did not function throughout the whole stoppage situation. Only the president of the board functioned. In the final analysis the mayor had to tell him what to do and call the whole board together to override this one man, who had created a rather rigid position. He really refused to negotiate or to bargain. He's an attorney for the shipping industry of New York City. I guess he thought he could use some of the hard management techniques and win.

"At one point most of the city administration sat with him for

180

something like 30 hours and put it to him very bluntly. They said either you find a way of running the school system without 50,000 teachers or you find a way of replacing these 50,000 teachers or you go down there and negotiate with them.

"All those hours the administration had to pound away, and finally when he still wouldn't move the whole Board of Education had to be called in and told that the school system was going to be wrecked unless they bought this package we had proposed.

"I would say that probably at the present time there is no real function for the Board of Education within the City of New York. The city administration is calling the shots on all important matters, not only budgetary but in such areas as community involvement. I can't think of any major decisions that will be made in the near future by the board and not by the city administration."

This interviewer sees no reason to doubt Albert Shanker's assertion of concern for the proper education of pupils. His dedication to the welfare of teachers is not inconsistent with a simultaneous concern for the improvement of instruction, especially for pupils in disadvantaged areas. Shanker himself says that the last six days of the stoppage were devoted to tying down non-money matters after all the teacher benefit clauses had been finally agreed upon. And anyone who has seen Albert Shanker with Bernard Donovan knows that this tough union leader has earned the unqualified respect of his equally tough superintendent.

IMPLICATIONS OF THE COMING
NEA-AFT MERGER

Myron Lieberman

A merger of the National Education Association and American Federation of Teachers will probably be negotiated in the near future. Such a move will have far-reaching national implications for teacher militancy. Perhaps because very few educators realize how imminent merger is, our professional literature is virtually devoid of any consideration of the likely conditions and consequences of merger. Inasmuch as organizational rivalry plays such an important role in teacher militancy, it would be unrealistic to consider the dynamics of teacher militancy without serious attention to the effects of merger upon it.

In the following comments, I am going to assume that merger will take place within a few years. This assumption is based largely upon what appears to me to be the practical logic of the situation. My purpose here, however, is not to demonstrate what appears obvious to me, i.e., that the merger will take place in the next few years at most, but to call attention and scholarly inquiry into what is problematical, the conditions and consequences of merger. These are the crucial problems, not whether or when the merger will occur.

Without question, the organizational rivalry between the NEA and AFT has been an important stimulus to teacher militancy. At all levels, the two organizations and their state and local affiliates have come under much more pressure to achieve benefits than would be the case if there were only one organization. A representation election almost invariably causes the competing organizations to adopt a more militant stance in order to demonstrate their effectiveness in achieving teacher goals. For the same reason, any failure to press vigorously for teacher objectives becomes a threat to organizational survival. State and national support are poured into local elections and negotiation sessions in order to protect the interests of the state and national affiliates. Thus at the local level organizational rivalry has led to a vastly greater organizational effort to advance teacher objectives. This development is consistent with the experience of competing organizations in other fields.

The crucial importance of the

PHI DELTA KAPPAN, November 1968, pp. 139-144.

NEA-AFT rivalry in stimulating teacher militancy raises the question of whether the merger of the two organizations will reduce such militancy. Probably, the merger will simultaneously encourage some tendencies toward greater teacher militancy and some toward less militancy; the overall outcome is likely to vary widely from district to district and time to time. To see why, it will be helpful to review the issues involved in merger.

Historically, two major organizational issues have divided the NEA and AFT. One was the fact that local, state, and national education associations typically permitted all-inclusive membership, i.e., these associations enrolled administrators and supervisors (hereafter referred to as "administrators" or "administrative personnel") as well as teachers. The other issue was the AFT's affiliation with the AFL-CIO. It is becoming evident, however, that these issues no longer divide the organizations as they did in the past.

In the first place, a number of teacher negotiation laws and/or state administrative agencies have settled the issue of administrator membership substantially along the lines advocated by the AFT. True, in a few other states, such as Connecticut, Washington, and Maryland, state negotiations legislation permits or even mandates the inclusion of administrative personnel in a teacher bargaining unit; but this aspect of the statutes is either ignored in practice or is creating too many practical difficulties for all parties. In any event, the Michigan experience is likely to be the predominant pattern. In that state,

many superintendents withdrew from, or did not join, local associations after passage of the Michigan negotiations statute in 1965. In 1966, the Michigan Association of School Administrators withdrew from the Michigan Education Association and joined with the Michigan School Boards Association and Michigan School Business Officials to form a new organization. In 1967, the state organizations of elementary and secondary school principals pulled out of the Michigan Education Association.

It should be noted that in the collective negotiations context, administrator membership in the teacher organization (which is not the same thing as membership in the same negotiating unit as teachers) is dangerous for the school board as well as for the teacher organization. Such membership, especially if the administrative personnel are active in the teacher organization, could lead to charges of employer support or domination of the employee (teacher) organization or to other unfair labor practices. In other words, administrator membership may jeopardize both the organization's right to represent teachers and the legitimacy of the board's approach to teacher bargaining.

The Michigan pattern concerning administrative membership in teacher organizations is still a minority one in the country as a whole. Nevertheless, it is likely to prevail eventually because of the difficulties inherent in maintaining all-inclusive membership in a negotiating organization. School boards will increasingly resist situations in which personnel assigned to administrative duties are represented by an organization controlled by the teachers they administer.

At the present time the issue of administrative membership is being debated at all organizational levels. In some districts the issue is seen as pertaining only to local organizations; it is assumed that administrative personnel can and should retain membership in state and national teacher organizations. In other places it is already accepted that administrative personnel cannot continue as regular members of local and state teacher organizations, but it is thought they should continue as members of NEA. Nevertheless, it is clear that even at the national level all-inclusive membership poses many sticky problems; the American Association of School Administrators, National Association of Secondary-School Principals, Department of Elementary School Principals, and Association for Supervision and Curriculum Development are some of the NEA departments already considering the need for modifying their relationships with the NEA in the near future.

The existence of these different approaches is understandable only in terms of intra-organizational perspectives. A state association leader might reluctantly accept the demise of all-inclusive membership at the local level but seek desperately to retain it at the state level. For one thing, he will naturally be unhappy at the prospect of losing dues revenue from administrators and supervisors. And if, as is often the case, such personnel play important roles in recruiting teachers to state membership, the loss of administrative personnel involves much more than the numbers of such personnel. In this situation the state association leader easily convinces himself that all-inclusive membership in the state association is still desirable. After all, he tells himself and others, the local association, not the state, is the negotiating organization. Furthermore, both teachers and administrators have a common interest in more state aid, an improved retirement system, and so on.

As plausible as these arguments are, they ignore the pressures toward separation at the state as well as at the local level. How will administrators be represented in the state association, if not through local associations? What will happen to administrators in districts too small to establish local organizations of administrators? Since the state organization will invariably support teachers in showdowns at the local level—to do otherwise would be organizational hara-kiri—how will administrators be able to work vigorously for their objectives inside the organization? How will school boards react to administrative membership in organizations supporting teachers' strikes or other militant action against the board and its representatives? Will administrators be willing to pay dues to state organizations that support teachers in militant anti-administration activities?

In their frantic efforts to maintain the status quo, some state association leaders have overlooked these hard questions relating to administrative membership in state teacher organizations. Nevertheless, administrators are taking the initiative in withdrawing from the state associations as often or more often than they are being excluded from them by militant teachers.

The same kind of wishful thinking characterized the outlook of NEA leaders until the recent past. For several reasons, NEA leaders did not want to adopt a position on administrative membership at local and state levels. There was concern that the exclusion of administrators from NEA would be damaging in terms of NEA membership, and again, the fear was related to administrative help in recruiting teacher members as well as to the loss of administrators per se. There was an emphasis upon the common interests of teachers and administrators at the national level, e.g., in getting more federal aid. There was also a failure to grasp the interdependence of local, state, and national organizations in a negotiating context.

An even more difficult problem was the tremendous regional, state, and local differences relating to negotiations. Association experience in Michigan or Massachusetts meant nothing to association leaders in Alabama or Mississippi. A membership policy vis-à-vis administrators that would have seemed sensible in Michigan would have horrified association members in Alabama.

The resolution of this difficult organizational problem was deceptively simple. The NEA's *Guidelines to Professional Negotiation* (1965) proposed that the inclusion of administrators in the negotiating unit and the negotiating organization be left to local option. This was not very helpful to local associations who wanted guidance on what their policy should be, but it was probably the only feasible way to avoid the issue until the pro-negotiation forces were stronger and there was a wider understanding of the problem throughout the association structure. Certainly, some NEA leaders realized from the outset of the negotiations movement that local option on administrator membership, without limits or guidelines, was a hopeless long-range policy; but a realistic policy had no chance of acceptance in the early 1960's.

A merger between the NEA and AFT will unquestionably accelerate the flight of administrative personnel from the merged organizations at all levels. First, the very fact that merger talks are taking place will confirm the feelings of many administrators that the associations are becoming "just like the union"—if not worse—and hence that administrators have no business in the association, with or without a merger. A more important point is that the AFT will demand some type of administrative exclusion as a condition of merger. Such a demand would actually make more sense from a propaganda than from a substantive point of view. The reason is that the inclusion of AFT membership in a new organization would tip the organizational balance in favor of administrative exclusion. Thus even if the exclusion of administrators were not a condition of merger, such exclusion would be organizational policy anyway within a year or two after merger. I suggest this independently of any conclusion about the desirability of excluding administrators from teacher organizations; the point is that a sincere belief in the importance of such exclusion does not necessarily justify setting it as a condition of merger.

Note that the issue here is not whether administrators have or should have the right to join teacher organizations. Most assuredly, they do have the right and will continue to have it, insofar as teachers permit it. The real issue is whether a teacher organization which includes administrators should have the legal right to represent teachers on terms and conditions of employment. Teachers and administrators have a constitutionally protected right to join the same organizations, but organizations enrolling both teachers and administrators do not have a constitutionally protected right to represent teachers in negotiations with their employers. Organizational rights to represent teachers are conditioned by law upon a number of public policy considerations. One such consideration is whether the organization can represent employees effectively. In private employment, this consideration has led to the mandatory exclusion of managerial personnel if the organization is to retain negotiating rights. The alleged differences between public and private employment, professional and nonprofessional employment, and between education and other fields are not likely to weaken the public policy arguments for exclusion of administrators from organizations seeking to represent teachers.

E xperience in other fields strongly suggests that administrative membership in state and national teacher organizations will probably not survive collective negotiations by teachers. If such membership is to survive, which is doubtful in any case, it is essential for the NEA and its affiliates to examine the issue by some sort of high-level task force in which teachers and administrators alike could have confidence. Such a task force would have to include experts in collective negotiations and public administration who clearly had no vested interest in the outcome and who could propose a feasible structure for all-inclusive membership. Otherwise, the forced exclusion or voluntary withdrawal of administrators from state associations and the NEA will increase rapidly, and the makeshift arrangements to hold everyone together will continue to ignore important practical considerations. One comprehensive study of the problem, adequately staffed and financed, would have served better than the hasty and improvised studies that have been made thus far. In any event, no task force of the kind envisaged has been or is in prospect; since such a group might well conclude that the separation is desirable and inevitable, perhaps little has been or will be lost by the absence of such an effort.

We should recognize, however, that many of the arguments for or against separation are oversimplifications of a complex problem. Teachers and administrators do not have to be in the same organization in order to communicate and cooperate with each other. Likewise, the fact that they are in the same organization would not necessarily reduce tensions or disagreements or conflicts between them. In other words, equating all-inclusive membership with cooperation, or separate organizations with conflict, is an oversimplification. In any case, the most probable outcome is a sort of confederation of educational organizations, in which each controls its own membership, budget, and policies. There could be joint financing and support of activities commanding the support of all organizations while the organizations go their own way in areas where their views or interests clash. Obviously, we can expect such clashes in the areas of collective negotiations and teacher militancy.

The upshot seems to me to be this: Regardless of the formal membership structure of the merged organization, teachers will control the state and national organizations that merge. The emerging organizations will put great pressure on teachers to join, and we can expect a dramatic increase in teacher organizational membership at all levels. With greatly increased membership and resources—none of which are needed to fight a rival teacher organization—and without the internal constraints inherent in administrator membership or control, the new organization will probably pursue more militant policies in behalf of teacher interests and views than anything we have experienced thus far in either NEA or AFT.

I say "probably" because some aspects of merger will tend to reduce teacher militancy. Thus it is often thought that merger will reduce teacher militancy by eliminating competition between the two organizations. So long as two organizations are competing for members, there is great pressure on each to achieve significant results. With merger, this pressure, and the militancy it generates, will disappear. Interestingly enough, many leaders

in both organizations, as well as experienced observers familiar with experience in other fields, share this expectation.

Undoubtedly, organizational rivalry typically results in greater organizational militancy. Even if this were not the case in other fields, it is clear that the recent sweeping changes in the NEA and its state and local affiliates would not have occurred (at least not so soon) except for the challenge of the AFT. This conclusion is not questioned, privately at least, by many NEA leaders.

Nevertheless, although organizational rivalry increases teacher militancy, it does not necessarily follow that merger will reduce such militancy, or that every aspect of merger will have this effect. For example, in many school districts, neither the local association nor the federation can afford full-time local leadership. With merger, the teachers may be able to support full-time local leadership with adequate facilities; much of the time and resources that were devoted to fighting the other teacher organization may now be directed at the school board. One of the certain consequences of merger will be a substantial increase in full-time representation of teachers and in their organizational resources, facilities, and support at all levels.

The increase in organizational capability may not fully offset the loss of dynamism inherent in two competing organizations. The crucial point, however, is that merger will not necessarily end the kind of competition and rivalry that has undergirded so much recent teacher militancy. In short, we must consider the possibility that competition *within* the merged organization will result in as much teacher militancy as competition between the present separate organizations.

I have noted that enrolling everyone in the same organization does not automatically eliminate differences or conflicts of interest among the members. In negotiations where there are rival organizations, the minority organization may criticize the results in order to persuade teachers to vote for and join the minority organization and give it a chance to become the bargaining agent. With one organization, the objective is to persuade teachers to change the leadership of the organization instead of to change their organizational affiliation. However, from the standpoint of teacher militancy, the dynamics of the situation can be much the same. In both situations, there is pressure on organizational leadership to achieve results, and there is also a leadership need to arouse teacher militancy for the same purpose.

The crucial difference between competition between two organizations and competition within a single organization relates to the capacity of those not in control of the organizational machinery to wage an effective campaign against the incumbents. To be specific, NEA publications are controlled by persons independent of AFT control, and vice versa. Thus, regardless of which organization is the bargaining agent in a given school district, there is a rival organizational apparatus not controlled by the bargaining agent. This rival apparatus constitutes a source of information, criticism, and opinion whose very existence places

greater pressure on the bargaining agent to achieve every possible gain.

If, however, there is a merger and therefore only one organization, how will critics and opponents of the incumbent leadership get their views publicized? They will no longer have an official organizational publication for this purpose. They will no longer control organizational conventions, conferences, news releases, and other means of disseminating their views. As a result, the incumbent leadership comes under less pressure to achieve results, with a consequent diminution of teacher militancy.

Merger per se will tend to weaken effective capacity to oppose incumbent leadership, and such weakening will inevitably lessen teacher militancy. However, appropriate action could be taken to insure that this does not happen. The appropriate action would be the introduction of the caucus system in the merged organization. Because the long-range effects of the merger will depend on how soon and how effectively caucuses are established in the new organization, and because the existence and effectiveness of caucuses will be the major influence on teacher militancy in the merged organization, it is necessary to analyze their role in some detail.

A caucus system is essentially a system of political parties within the organization. Organization members may join a caucus, pay dues to it, attend its meetings, participate in its deliberations, and perhaps represent it in official organization proceedings. It is essential that caucuses be financed and operated independently of the organizational machinery; otherwise there is the danger that the caucus will lose its ability to function as an independent source of information, criticism, and leadership. The crucial point is that in the absence of a caucus, individual members or convention delegates are helpless before the organizational machinery. To change organizational policy or to launch a campaign to change organizational leadership, collective action is needed. First, there must be a forum not controlled by incumbent leadership in which the opposition has full opportunity to state its case and generate support. Floor fights (hopefully, only verbal ones) must be organized, fall-back positions established, and strategy coordinated. Signs, posters, and other literature may have to be printed and disseminated, and so on. These and other essentials of effective organizational leadership or influence cannot be initiated effectively by ad hoc committees or organizations, which are formed—usually over one issue—at a particular convention and then wither away. At all times there must be an organizational mechanism which can serve all the constructive purposes served by a rival organization. Such a mechanism, however, must be as independent of control by incumbent leadership as is a rival organization.

The incumbent leadership will also need a political mechanism independent of the organizational machinery. The elected officers of the organization should not be able to use organizational funds to finance their election campaign. As in most such situations, the incumbents will have certain political advantages accruing from their incumbency, but they too will have political needs which cannot legitimately be met by using official organizational machinery. It would, therefore, be erroneous to regard caucuses solely as a means for helping the "out's" clobber the "in's." Neither democracy nor militancy will flourish in the merged organization unless there exists practical means of exerting organizational influence and leadership which are not dependent upon the official organizational structure. Policies and leaders must be forged in the caucuses, and thence into the official organizational structure. If this is done, and I believe it can and must be done, we can be optimistic about the level of internal democracy in the merged organization. We can also expect a continuing high level of teacher militancy under these conditions.

AFFILIATION AS A MERGER ISSUE

For all practical purposes, the forthcoming merger will end teacher affiliation with the AFL-CIO. The AFT will need some face-saving concession on this issue, such as a national referendum on the question within the merged organization or local option to affiliate with the AFL-CIO; but the issue is already a dead horse for all practical reasons. The fact that AFT leaders are already proposing a referendum, knowing full well that it would be overwhelmingly defeated in the merged organization, ought to be signal enough for anyone to see. There is even reason to doubt whether such a referendum confined to the present AFT membership would support affiliation. Certainly there is very little sentiment in the AFT to insist upon affiliation at the cost of preventing merger.

Allowing local option to affiliate with the AFL-CIO might be a viable solution, since it would ease the transition problem, support the principle of local autonomy, and quickly lead to disaffiliation anyway. Affiliation with the AFL-CIO is not important to most AFT members, but it is important to some AFT leaders in some large urban centers. If local option is permitted, only a few locals will affiliate with the AFL-CIO, and the impracticalities of such a relationship will lead to their disaffiliation soon afterward. Furthermore, it is doubtful whether the AFL-CIO would find it advantageous to enroll a few teacher locals, even a few relatively large ones.

Since the teacher organizations choosing to be affiliated with the AFL-CIO would not be a rival to the merged teacher organizations, affiliation would not constitute an organizational issue as it does now. Actually, there is no constitutional reason now why an NEA local affiliate cannot affiliate with the AFL-CIO. Such affiliation would probably lead to expulsion by the NEA Executive Committee under present circumstances, but such a reaction would be overkill if there were only one teacher organization. At any rate, despite the enormous importance of the issue in the propaganda war between NEA and AFT, it is not a very important substantive issue, and it will not hold up merger as long as it takes to read this paper.

What will be the impact of disaffiliation on teacher militancy? A popular view is that AFT militancy is due to its affiliation with the AFL-CIO. This seems very questionable. Affiliation has contributed to AFT militancy, in specific communities under specific circumstances; likewise, affiliation has often been a conservative influence in many situations. The teacher stereotype of labor bosses inciting teachers to strike is far removed from the facts, as is the notion that the AFT depends largely upon the AFL-CIO or the IUD [Industrial Union Department, whose main function is recruitment] for support. The AFL-CIO did play an important role in the early stages of the AFT's drive for collective bargaining, but it is not a decisive factor now. Surely, there have been enough teacher strikes, boycotts, sanctions, and other pressures by associations in recent years to end the fallacy that affiliation with the AFL-CIO underlies or is an essential ingredient of teacher militancy. In fact, nonteacher members of the AFL-CIO at any level may view teachers' strikes more critically as parents and taxpayers than favorably as the justified efforts of fellow wage earners. Realistically, there is no strong reason to believe that disaffiliation will reduce teacher militancy in any significant way.

The major problems of merger are not philosophical or ideological; they are practical, such as who gets what job in the merged organization. The practical problems will be complicated more by the political implications of any settlement than by the equities from a strictly organizational or employment point of view. To be candid, there are enough resources to take care of everybody reasonably well. The more difficult problems will arise over the inevitable efforts by the negotiators on both sides to place their political supporters in as many of the key positions as possible. These efforts will create internal problems on each side which may be more difficult to resolve than the issues dividing the negotiators along organizational lines.

It would be naive to underestimate the importance of this problem. Beyond the broad social factors affecting teacher militancy, the quality of teacher leadership is necessarily a crucial factor in the dynamics and future of teacher militancy. For this reason, my concluding comments will relate to this matter.

The most immediate effects of merger upon leadership will be at the state level. In a number of states, federation locals dominate the large urban districts, whereas other districts are largely association-dominated. Especially where the AFT-dominated districts include greater proportions of all the teachers in the state, the impact of merger may be truly traumatic at the state level. In fact, there are states where federation members have no significant reservations about affiliation at the national level but object strenuously to state association leadership. This is especially true in states like California and Minnesota, where state association leadership—to the obvious chagrin of many NEA leaders—has vigorously opposed effective negotiation legislation.

Another point here is that the NEA's national staff is much more oriented to collective negotiations and teacher militancy than is the leadership of many state associations. Many state associations are oriented more to lobbying in the state legislature than to effective support of locals at the bargaining table. It appears that the NEA has had to establish regional field offices to assist local associations in negotiations partly because of state association slowness in responding to the negotiations movement. The state associations in Massachusetts, Michigan, New Jersey, and Rhode Island were the quickest to adapt effectively to negotiations, but in many states the local associations must still look to the NEA rather than the state association for significant help in negotiations. Indeed, this is still necessary occasionally in the states mentioned as having made the most rapid adjustment. The point is, however, that merger will sometimes change the constituency of the state organization more than it will the national; hence changes in leadership and policy in some of the state organizations may emerge rather quickly.

At the national level, full-time leadership in the merged organization will be largely as it is now in the NEA, at least for the near future. This is not only due to the arithmetic of the situation, i.e., the NEA's much greater membership and national staff. It will also be due to the fact that most of the NEA's present leadership is negotiation-oriented. Merger, therefore, will not be seen as a threat but as a step forward toward a more militant organization. On this score, it must be conceded that changes in the NEA within the past few years, and especially since its top leadership changed in 1967, have been truly remarkable.

In the early 1960's, one New York City law firm (Kaye, Scholer, Fierman, Hays, and Handler) provided the national leadership and the expertise which saved the NEA and its affiliates from organizational catastrophe in its competition with the AFT. It is a little known but singular fact that a New York City law firm, which ordinarily represents management in its labor practice, negotiated the first association agreements, trained the association staff, and guided the NEA to an acceptance of, and commitment to, collective negotiations. Ironically, corporation lawyers succeeded in convincing NEA leadership (correctly, it appears) that the NEA had to cease rejecting collective negotiations and demonstrate its determination to negotiate better agreements for teachers than those negotiated by the AFT. As this view prevailed, those who supported it became more influential in the NEA; today, NEA leadership is clearly committed to collective negotiations and includes a capability in this area which is not inferior to the federation's.

Without getting into personalities therefore, it seems to me that one of the most encouraging aspects of the present situation is the tremendous improvement in the quality of teacher leadership and in the likelihood that merger will strengthen the tendencies in this direction. If this is the case, teacher militancy will continue to increase and will be increasingly devoted to constructive public policy as well as teacher objectives.

Mr. Superintendent,
I Want a Position as—

By
JOHN B. CROSSLEY

SERVICE TO TEACHERS is certainly one of the first responsibilities of the superintendent of schools. This responsibility begins with the day the teacher is employed and continues throughout the total period of service. Perhaps today's administrator should extend still earlier a service to teachers. This article is such an attempt, and carries to the teacher advice on securing a position—a step necessary prior to any additional service the superintendent may render his teachers.

The growth of enrollments in public schools throughout the nation has been repeatedly reported. The need for more teachers is critical. That this need is known nationally is evidenced by the number of teacher applications received annually by administrators in school districts from coast to coast. Perhaps more than the usual number of applications are received by those superintendents fortunate enough to be located in regions where climatic and salary conditions induce teachers from less desirable localities to seek employment in the more favored districts.

Charged with the responsibility for locating and employing teachers, the superintendent and his staff devote much time and serious consideration to applications and letters of inquiry concerning vacancies.

Such inquiries are welcomed, and provision is made for immediate and full consideration of the applicants. But—too often—the applicant removes most chance for serious consideration through his approach.

For example: If you were a superintendent of schools anxious to employ superior teachers, how would you react to the following samples of letters of inquiry?

1. This letter, typed carelessly, without reference to proper form of a good letter:

My Dear Superintendent—

They say they are short of teachers in California, so if you are needing an industrial Arts Teacher or one with a social sciences Minor, and can use a man of the fifties who has been certified for Smith-Hughes Shop in Illinois, and Michigan and had much teaching experience in Iowa; and can use a Presbyterian, married, why not get in touch with me here.

(My reaction: After a third reading, tempted to "get in touch." On first reading —carelessness, lack of skill in one of the three R's, poor judgment exemplified by the quality and nature of the inquiry. Direct letter to the wastebasket!)

2. This letter, written with green pencil in longhand and with careless penmanship:

Dear Sirs:

I am interested in a Science, and Driver Education position in your schools.

Cheerily Yours,

THE CLEARING HOUSE, November 1957, pp. 140-143.

(My reaction: So glad to know writer is "cheery"—but carelessness and poor judgment give little incentive to put into motion all that is necessary to secure further information. To the "round file.")

3. This introductory paragraph, in a letter neatly typed, followed by a brief résumé of experience and training:

I am interested in obtaining complete information about your school system and the cost of living in your community. I am considering moving to the West Coast at the end of the current school year. I would appreciate information concerning salary schedule, tenure, class load, extracurricular activities, and housing costs.

(My reaction: Which comes first—the service a teacher can render via training and experience, the desire to serve youth—or salary, security, relative difficulty or ease of assignment? I put the former first and react negatively to one who asks first "what salary?" and "what working conditions?" Forget this one!)

4. This introductory paragraph in a letter carelessly typed on the stationery of the school where the applicant was then employed:

Superintendent of City Schools:

I am moving to California to work in the school system. In view of this, I should like having some information relative to the following: teacher retirement, salary schedule, possibility of employment in your system, and any other information you should deem helpful to me.

(My reaction: Much as in the example immediately above. The applicant here again is asking for information "helpful" to him—with no evidence he in turn could be helpful to our students. Discard!)

5. These portions from several letters give samples too often found:

Because we, as a family, have decided to move to a warmer climate. . . .

. . . I feel we would like to change to a location near the seashore. . . .

I would welcome the change of residence since my wife, who is "expecting" in September, would like to be closer to her parents and close friends.

(My reaction: None of the above letters, as is generally the case when such statements are included, gave added information in sufficient detail to identify those qualifications of the applicant to teach or to suggest interest in serving students above a desire for a more favorable climate or location. Let's not waste time on these!)

6. These written on two-penny post cards —two in longhand, difficult to read due to poor penmanship, one carelessly typed:

Please send me copies of your salary schedules for secondary teachers and counselors.

Will you mail me a contract, stating salary, via *Air Mail* at once to start teaching in your schools on a junior high school or general secondary credential?

Dear Supt.

I should like to secure a position teaching MUSIC(Band-Orchestra-Piano-Vocal-etc) in your system. Below my qualifications are briefly listed. Please advise me if a possible position exists for which I may apply.
DEGREE: *Masters*(Columbia Univ);BA(San Jose Univ)
MAJORS: *Music*
FIELDS: *Band-Orchestra-Piano-Vocal-etc.Strings*
EXPERIENCE: five(5) years; secondary, college
SUBJECTS TAUGHT: Band-Orchestra-Chorus-Piano(Class and private lessons); instrumental instruction; Theory, Elementary Music;Baton Whirling etc. I shall consider any type of music instruction. May I hear from you?

(My reaction: Is the use of a postal card indicative of a somewhat offhand interest in a position, of lack of appreciation of the importance and dignity of the teaching profession? Could be? Let's not "dignify" these by a response. Discard!)

Should the administrator recognize through the use of ingenious methods of inquiry a quality of imagination valuable in a good teacher and thus follow with a like response to the following types of applications?

1. The receipt of a page of the classified advertisement section of a metropolitan newspaper, upon which is pasted—over the "position wanted" section—the following printed statements:

194

Are you in Need of a Teacher? . . . Particular Whom You Hire?

EXPERIENCED TEACHER, highly recommended and versatile, available for secondary school position in drama, English, or journalism. This 32-yr-old male, interested in the fine arts, seeks a community desirable for permanent residence. Don't let late application fool you. Papers at ——— Teacher Placement.

2. A letter of inquiry with the following opening paragraphs in "poetic" style:

Searching for a new beginning for a letter is like seeking another job, I believe. It is there, however difficult it may be to position it.

That is my plight, somewhat in fright, for I see nothing in sight. Be it early, or uncertain, surely you would not consider it inadvertent if I inquire if you need someone for hire.

This is but in brief, please turn to the next leaf. Presently teaching Algebra I, General Mathematics, General Science, and Physical Education and coaching Football, Boxing, and Track.

(My reaction: Yes, we do appreciate imagination and ingenuity in our teachers. But to start off with a display of these traits might indicate that in time, should they grow, they might get out of hand. Better not take time on these!)

Do the following deserve reply, or do they identify a basic lack of the qualities desired in candidates for teaching positions?

1. A mimeographed page giving an outline of training and experience and at the top of the page simply the statement—in longhand and with no salutation—"Interested in teaching commerce," and at the bottom of the page simply the name and address of the applicant added in longhand.

2. A mimeographed letter reporting interest in and qualifications for a position including a sharp criticism of the school where the applicant was then employed—this to explain why he was interested in making a change.

(My reaction: Much as in the case of the postal-card inquiries. If one is serious about the position sought, considers the position important, classifies teaching as

worthy of quality effort and training, use of the cheapest quality of paper and duplicating letters makes the recipient wonder. Cast aside!)

What mystery lies behind the receipt of the two letters which follow—both written by the same applicant? The first letter was neatly typed, the name of the superintendent to whom it was addressed was used, a self-addressed stamped envelope was enclosed.

I am seeking a job in your locality as a high school teacher of mathematics, to begin in September, 1955.

I will graduate from the ——— University in June of this year with a B.S. degree in education (major: Mathematics; minor: social studies), and plan to start working for an M.S. degree this summer. I am a Navy veteran, aged 24, in excellent health, married, with one child.

If you are interested in my qualifications, I will gladly request the University to furnish you with my full credentials. Whether you know of an opening or not, I should appreciate your reply.

The second letter was dated twenty days later. It was written carelessly in longhand. Errors in English usage, spelling, and punctuation will be noted—its whole tone was different from the first.

Dear Sir:

I am interested in moving west because I believe there Philosophy of Education more nearly like mine. The west is growing and I want to grow with it. I like your climate and would very much like to live and learn and produce in your state.

A photograph can be obtained along with my credentials which are on call with the Teachers Placement Bureau. . . .

Since I am a married man and we are excepting our second child in Sept. I feel I can't except a position for less than $3400. If you believe I am worth the expense please send for my credentials or write me and I'll have the college send them.

The first letter was answered, and an application form was forwarded the applicant. The completed application accompanied the second letter, though no reference was made to it. Rightly or wrongly, the second letter removed all interest in the candidate.

That the foregoing samples of letters of application or inquiry are not unique can be verified by many administrators. No common pattern of training is exemplified in the writers. The letters are from both experienced and inexperienced teachers, and are from those trained in colleges and universities from coast to coast. That some of these letters were written by very able teachers cannot be denied. The ability to write a good letter of application certainly is not a valid criterion upon which to judge completely an applicant's teaching ability.

However, there certainly is a reaction—a first impression gained—to a letter written to one who is a complete stranger. This is especially true when the writer is requesting the reader to give serious consideration to one who should meet acceptable standards of good taste, who should demonstrate satisfactory mastery of the elementary skills of a well-written letter—penmanship, spelling, and English usage. Through his letter, the applicant must convey qualities which would lead the administrator to provide the time and expense of offering the services of the school district in setting into motion the complicated procedures of teacher selection.

With teachers desperately needed, the administrator is most eager to give every consideration to applications. A letter of inquiry stating interest in a position, identifying briefly training and experience, and giving a favorable impression of the writer, at least through a neat, correct, and businesslike letter is welcome. It will bring a request for more information and a response from the administrator defining positions available, the procedure of application, details of salary and working conditions—for he, too, has a selling job to do if he is to secure the most qualified instructors for the schools of his district.

To applicants, then, this appeal: If you write a letter of application, remember that the administrator who receives it wants to know that you are trained for the position you seek, have exact or related experience for the job, have a real interest in teaching, hold or can secure necessary teaching credentials or certificates, and have reason to believe you can serve students well. If you provide him this knowledge through a careful and correct letter, he will respond quickly and provide the information you seek.

In composing your letter of inquiry:

Don't emphasize your interest in: salary schedule, security, climate, ease of assignment, length of school day.

Do emphasize your interest in: teaching, serving youth.

Do: use standard quality of paper, write in correct letter style, use correct English, spell accurately, write legibly or type carefully, use correct name or title of administrator if you have the information available, enclose a self-addressed, stamped envelope if you request a reply.